HYMNS OF A TRAVELER

Lewis Codington

PREFACE

I love the old hymns. They are filled with powerful messages of our Christian beliefs. Some of them, I associate with my long gone parents... and I can still hear them singing certain hymns. Some I connect with my wife and can recall her singing in our college days. Many have endured and remained popular for hundreds of years. But in addition to the hymns themselves, I also really love reading about the stories behind the hymns. Quite a few were written out of terrible tragedies, reminding us that God can and does bring good out of suffering and hardship. Some were written by seemingly unknown and inconsequential individuals, also reminding us that God uses ordinary people to spread his Message of hope and salvation. I trust you will enjoy these stories and be encouraged in your faith.

I am so grateful for my parents, Herbert A. and Page L. Codington, whose enthusiasm and gusto in singing embedded these hymns in my mind.

LC
Lookout Mountain, Tennessee
2023

INDEX OF HYMNS

1 - HOLY, HOLY, HOLY

On a trip to Bangladesh in the 1970s, I remember visiting a church dedicated by Reginald Heber, the author of the hymn, "Holy, Holy, Holy". "Wow!", I thought, "that great hymnwriter was a missionary in this far off corner of Asia?!? Amazing!" Heber was born in Cheshire, England, in 1783. Soon after completing his education, Reginald was ordained in the Anglican Church and served in a small church in the village of Hodnet. Reginald developed a reputation for being a devoted follower of God and a wonderful poet - which was the perfect recipe for an enduring hymn. In 1823, Reginald was called to serve in India. He became the Bishop of Calcutta, which made him leader over missions in India, Ceylon, and Australia. During his time in India, Reginald worked tirelessly to build a training school for local clergy so the area would have ministers for the long term. Reginald also traveled across India spreading the Gospel. Over the years, the climate and his heavy responsibilities wore on Reginald's health. One Sunday, after an outdoor sermon to a large gathering, Reginald dropped dead from heatstroke. Over the years he had written a number of hymns, which he never sought publication for. But his wife saw the beauty in her husband's work, and she put a collection of his hymns together and had them published. Fifty-seven hymns were included, one of which stood out far above the others: "Holy, holy, holy, Lord God Almighty!", which the author Alfred Lord Tennyson considered to be the greatest hymn ever written. I recall my Dad loving it as well. Heber's hymns have been a blessing to many for 200 years.

2 - RISE UP, O MEN OF GOD

A hymn which encourages us to work for the Lord while we wait for His return is "Rise Up, O Men of God". It was written by William Merrill, who was born in Orange, New Jersey, in 1867. He was a member of a Dutch Reformed Church in New Brunswick, NJ, and he wrote his first book, "Faith Building", in 1885, when he was just eighteen. After studying at Rutgers and Union Theological Seminary, he pastored churches in Philadelphia and Chicago. In 1896 he married Clara Helmer, and in 1900 authored his second book, "Faith and Sight". In 1911, Nolan R. Best, editor of a Presbyterian newspaper, suggested to Merrill that there was an urgent need of a "brotherhood hymn". About that same time, Merrill read an article by Gerald Stanley Lee entitled "The Church of the Strong Men". With these two ideas incubating in his mind, a hymn suddenly came to Merrill one day as he was returning to Chicago on a Lake Michigan steamer. The hymn challenges every child of God to rise up and serve the Lord. It was published in "The Pilgrim Hymnal" in 1912. In 1911, Merrill become minister of the Brick Presbyterian Church in New York City, where he remained until his retirement in 1938. In addition to preaching and producing hymns, he was the author of several more books.

3 - AMAZING GRACE

The one hymn I associate with my father the most is "Amazing Grace", which is interesting to me because, being a rather holy and pious individual, at least to me, I don't think of him as being someone who needed a whole lot of amazing grace. But if there was one person who did recognize emphatically that he needed a boatload of grace, it was John Newton, who penned the words of this hymn. Born in London in the early 1700s, into a family with a mother who prayed regularly for him, and who hoped he would become a pastor, Newton took a different path. He went to sea, and eventually became a slave trader. But he remembered his mother's prayers, and in the midst of a violent storm, during which his ship came frightfully close to sinking, he suddenly realized how greatly in need he was of God's grace. He began seriously delving into the Bible, and eventually became a well known pastor in England, also writing many hymns. Shortly before his death, by this time having only a dim memory, Newton spoke these words: "My memory is nearly gone, but I remember two things: that I am a great sinner, and that Christ is a great Savior." He had these words carved into his gravestone in his church yard: "John Newton, once an infidel and libertine, a servant of slaves in Africa, was, by the rich mercy of our Lord and Savior, Jesus Christ, preserved, restored, pardoned, and appointed to preach the faith he had long labored to destroy."

4 - ALL HAIL THE POWER OF JESUS' NAME

This hymn has an interesting and perhaps unlikely story attached to it. Edward Perronet grew up in the home of an Anglican vicar in the 1700s. After some time in the Anglican Church, he became fed up with them and joined the Methodists. During his time with this group, Perronet was roughed up, tossed around, dumped in the mud, and had stones thrown at him. But he had a falling out with the Methodists and moved on to another group...which he eventually left as well. Nevertheless, Perronet wrote this beautiful hymn, which became very loved in the church. It also became well utilized by evangelists and missionaries. One amazing missions story attached to the song is the following: "Reverend E. P. Scott was a missionary in India during the 1800s. At the prompting of the Holy Spirit, but against advice of his fellow missionaries, Scott set out alone to visit a remote village. He was determined to share the Gospel with a dangerous savage tribe. Several days into his journey. Scott met a large group of warriors who quickly surrounded him, each one pointing a spear towards his heart. Expecting to die, Scott made a decision to use his last few breaths to glorify God, and to hopefully stir something within the hearts of his captors. He took out his violin (which he always carried with him), closed his eyes, and began to play and sing 'All Hail the Power of Jesus' Name', in the native language of the warriors. After singing the first verse, the second, the third, and then beginning the fourth, Rev. Scott realized he was still standing, and that all around him was a peaceful quiet. Opening his eyes he saw every spear lowered. There stood those mighty warriors, with tears in their eyes. Throughout the remainder of his life, Scott spent much time with this tribe, sharing the love of God."

5 - LOVE DIVINE, ALL LOVES EXCELLING

Charles Wesley was truly the epic hymn writer for the church, having written some 6,000 hymns that we know of, nearly 300 years ago. How in the world did he do it? Well, it helps that, back in those pre-automobile days, everywhere he went was by horseback. So, while CW traipsed across the countryside as an itinerant preacher, he spent hours in the saddle...which was time well spent, often writing hymns based on Scripture that he had been reading. The words to this hymn are particularly remarkable, because Charles and his brother John were often scorned and ridiculed for their style and preaching content. They were even persecuted for their unorthodox ways that were outside of the ways of the traditional church. So, as much as he suffered, I find it surprising that Wesley could write about God's love, compassion, and mercy. Why would God allow all this suffering? And how could CW even write these words? Apparently, he understood well that he was undeserving of God's love. And, as our pastor reminded us this morning, God uses what is terrible and what he hates...to accomplish what he loves. Amazing thought...amazing truth. And our pastor is right...because hundreds of years later, we are still being greatly blessed by Wesley's hymns, in spite of all he suffered.

6 - IMMORTAL, INVISIBLE, GOD ONLY WISE

Walter Chalmers Smith was a minister in the Church of Scotland in the 1800s. In addition to bouncing around between a number of churches over several decades, he was also a writer of books, a poet, and a hymn writer. His hymn that we are most familiar with is this one: "Immortal, Invisible, God Only Wise". As we read the words, we are impressed with the staggering greatness of God, who is eternal, almighty, the giver of life...and a few other staggering descriptors. But what caught my attention, and is easy to miss in all the grandeur, is that this amazingly great God who is way beyond our comprehension...is full of love for us, love for you and me. Now that is truly something to dwell on, to feast on today!

7 - O, WORSHIP THE KING

This magnificent hymn was penned by a rather honorable man, Sir Robert Grant, a member of Parliament, the King's Sargent in the Court of the Duchy of Lancaster, a Director of the East India Company, and the Governor of Bombay...(whew!). But we remember him for writing this hymn. I especially appreciated it after reading 1 Kings 8 in my devotions, which tells of Solomon leading the people of God in worship. The hymn seemed to express in song the sentiments shared in this prayer of King Solomon to God...communicating to us God's greatness as he is omnipotent, trustworthy, infinite in love for us, too great to be contained in the universe, ever present with us, a giver of rest and joy to us. As the hymn declares, those words of Solomon leave us in worship of our great King.

8 - THERE'S A WIDENESS IN GOD'S MERCY

I don't think I ever realized it before, but apparently, a couple of hundred years ago in England, there was a fairly intense rivalry or tug of war between the Anglican Church and the Roman Catholic Church. Maybe that's an incorrect depiction, but it seems that there was a good bit of accusation and finger-pointing going on between them. There certainly are some similarities between the two: the use of liturgy, for example, and a high view of the sacraments. In some circles there may have even appeared to be little difference between the churches. At any rate, some church leaders were torn between the two. One such Anglican Vicar, who later converted to Catholicism, was Frederick Faber. Whatever internal struggles he may have experienced, he did get one thing right in his portrayal of God's vast and great mercy, which he expressed in this beautiful hymn.

9 - THIS IS MY FATHER'S WORLD

As we sang about "Our Father's World" this morning, I was humbled at the thought that our Heavenly Father, who rules over all things, has allowed us to take on the roles of fathers as well... and, as such, to be examples to the world, and most of all to our own families, of what it means to be a selfless father, who lays down his life for his own. It also fascinates me to read the stories behind these hymns. Wouldn't it be great if we also, every time we go out to walk or run, would have the thought, "I'm going out to see my Father's world."? When Maltbie Babcock lived in Lockport, he took frequent walks along the area surrounding Niagara Falls, to enjoy the overlook's panoramic vista of New York state and around Lake Ontario, and telling his wife he was "going out to see his Father's world". She published a poem by Babcock shortly after his death, entitled "This is My Father's World", which became the hymn we still sing today.

10 - TAKE MY LIFE AND LET IT BE

As I think back over some of my favorite hymns, it is interesting, really, how they express such differing messages. Some talk about God's greatness, others about the wonders of his creation, still others talk about his power, his love, his grace, his peace which he extends to us, his mercy... This one, which we sang this morning in an Anglican Church in Nashville, on the occasion of our grandson's baptism, is more of a prayer... a beautiful prayer that offers oneself fully to God. The stories behind these hymns also fascinate me very much, because nearly always they are penned out of a crucial moment in the writer's journey through life. In the case of this one, Frances Havergal, a well known British hymn writer, reached a point in her life when she realized the need to totally dedicate her life, her whole self, to God.

11 - ALAS! AND DID MY SAVIOR BLEED

Isaac Watts was a rather amazing character on any scale (except in appearance, as he was all of five feet tall). At the time of his birth, his father was in prison for being a "dissenter" from the Anglican Church in England. Isaac learned Latin at age four, picked up Greek by age nine, and Hebrew at 13. As a teenager, he was frustrated with the tedious music of the church, so his father challenged him to do better. He responded by setting out on a hymn writing frenzy, eventually composing 600 of the best known hymns, mostly written in his teens and twenties! Eventually, Watts became known as the "Father of English Hymnody". This hymn, "Alas! And Did my Savior Bleed", spoke powerfully and convictingly to the blind Fanny Crosby 100 years later, and she then became a great hymn writer herself.

12 - COME, THOU FOUNT OF EVERY BLESSING

I doubt if anyone else has this problem, but sometimes I wake up in the middle of the night feeling anxious about this or that situation I imagine. When that happens, I try to take it as an invitation from God to spend time with him, singing hymns or praying. When I sing the old hymns I remember from my boyhood, I try to see how far I can get, starting with an "A" hymn (Amazing Grace, All the Way my Savior Leads me…), then a "B" one (Blessed Assurance, Because he Lives), and down through the alphabet. Well, last night I woke up again, and began singing. But I got stuck on "C"…I just couldn't think of any "C" hymns during the night. The very first hymn we sang this morning at church was this one, a "C" hymn! The funny thing about this hymn, though, is that, just as I was confused trying to think of a "C" hymn, there may be some confusion about this song. The story below is fascinating… but is it true? What makes it so confusing is that apparently there were two Robert Robinsons living at the same time in England in the 1700s! Both were dissenters from the state church. It seems a little unclear about who wrote this hymn and if the story is even true. (Hopefully, one of my more knowledgeable ancient hymn expert friends can clarify this mystery for us.) At any rate, what struck me this morning was the phrase, "Tune my heart to sing thy praise". It hit me that as followers of God, when we sometimes get off track or down in the dumps, it may be because we get "out of tune" with God. So it's very appropriate for us to ask God to put our hearts and lives back in tune with him! I love that idea. (And hopefully I'll remember this "C" hymn next time I awake early...)

13 - LET US LOVE, AND SING, AND WONDER

We lived in China for seven years, and I have to admit that I did pretty poorly at grasping the language. Although I did learn some of the Chinese characters…let's face it, it's a pretty daunting task when they have something like 50,000 characters (compared to 26 letters in the English alphabet!). But there was no doubt which character was my favorite…this one here: (義). Basically, it contains the entire Message of the Good News of God in one character. I loved it so much that I asked our carpenter (who previously had made our beds and tables) to carve it on a wooden plaque for us. So what does this character mean? It really is made up of two characters: "lamb" on top, and "me" below that. The two characters combined produce the character for "righteous". Why is that's so amazing? Because when the Lamb covers me, it makes me righteous In God's eyes. I was so excited about it that I wanted to, a bit prematurely, granted, go ahead and have our grave stone made so we could include that character on it!

Perhaps John Newton, when he penned the hymn nearly 300 years ago, had this same Chinese character in mind. He sounded excited, in the words of the hymn, over the fact that Christ's perfect sacrifice on our behalf has made us and our sinfulness washed away and clean before God. The old commandments that showed us our inadequacy and inability to save ourselves, are now pushed aside, when Christ's sacrifice is applied to our lives. Now, when God looks down at us, from heaven, all he sees is the righteousness of the Lamb that covers us and makes us righteousness. That's amazing grace for you!

14 - BENEATH THE CROSS OF JESUS

Do you sometimes wonder what heaven will be like? Many times we hear people say something like: "When I get to heaven, I'm going to do this, this, and this..." I jokingly say to people who help me out in some way, "I'll repay you by inviting you over for coffee when we get to heaven!" But it does all remain something of a mystery to us, doesn't it. One thing I am fairly certain about, however...we will be in for some big, interesting, pleasant surprises! Let me tell you about one such surprise. Have you ever heard the name, Elizabeth Clephane? Neither have I...and understandably so. Miss Elizabeth lived a brief life of 39 years in Scotland in the mid-1800s. Her parents died in her youth, and this shy woman endured an obscure life in ill health, trying to encourage people as she was able. She also composed a handful of hymns, most long forgotten. But two we remember, including the one, "Beneath the Cross of Jesus". It was published after her death, which most likely hardly anyone even noticed. I copied those words to the hymn out of a book I have been reading as I've been driving across the country this week from Phoenix, and through New Mexico, Texas, Oklahoma, Kansas, Missouri, and finally up to

Chicago, where, Lord willing, we will arrive today. I'm with our fourth son, in his nearly 20 year old Toyota, stuffed to the gills with all his stuff, plus room for our bodies to contort ourselves into. He is starting a new job in the big city, so I thought I would tag along for the ride. Anyway, back to the story... The book (which has very patiently sat on my shelves for 20 or 30 years, just waiting for me to lovingly embrace it), has finally been picked up by me for this trip. It is the gripping, unsettling account of a well known Bulgarian pastor, who suffered unimaginably in prison for 13 years under his Communist comrades. What helped to sustain him through this horrible experience? You guessed it...unknown Miss Elizabeth's now famous hymn. Singing it to himself, as well as to fellow sufferers, helped them all survive their harrowing ordeal. It's stunning to think about... and is a reminder to us that all of our lives, our examples, our acts done for Christ...will likely follow us in ways we cannot fully fathom. I can just picture the Bulgarian pastor, Haralan Popov, upon stepping through the Pearly Gates of the Celestial City, running to embrace Miss Elizabeth and recounting the story to her of how her precious words, 100 years later, in a far off Communist prison cell, sustained scores of folks she never could have imagined in her brief sojourn on earth! Isn't that amazing to think about?? What unexpected stories await us on high? I can't wait to hear them! (Well, in my case, I hope there are at least one or two…) But it's amazing to ponder how God uses and multiplies our feeble, humble sowing to bring in his harvest and extend his kingdom. What a day of rejoicing that will be…when we see Jesus face to face!

15 - ROCK OF AGES

One phrase that was embedded into our brains in England during the ten years we lived there was something you would see posted in the subways and trains everywhere. And our good pastor in Tennessee apparently has visited England as well, because he reminded us of it in our church service this morning, as he shared about Jacob in Genesis 35. It is the phrase: "Mind the gap". Quite understandably, when we prepare to hop onto a train or subway, we do need to mind the gap, unless we plan to get clobbered and crushed by the speeding vehicle. Our pastor made the good point of how a gap also separated Jacob's less than stellar life and behavior...and God's mercy and good plans in and through him...and us, which way surpass any anemic efforts we may produce.

But I also was reminded of this same gap in one of the hymns that was played in the service: "Rock of Ages". This hymn was written by the exotically named Augustus Toplady, who worked himself to death at the very early age of 38. But before that happened, in addition to composing this beautiful hymn, Mr. Toplady created quite a gap in his own life. Differing theologically from Charles Wesley, the man who gave us a never ending flow of wonderful hymns, Toplady had the audacity of equating Wesley with the devil, and succeeded quite well at alienating not a few other friends as well. Still, remarkably, God used Mr. A.T. to bless endless generations of folks who came after him with the beautiful and profound words of this hymn. In addition to both men, Toplady and Wesley, bringing us incalculable blessing, they bring home to us the reality that, in spite of the glaring gaps in our own lives, God chooses to use us in his grand eternal plans anyway. Isn't that wonderful news for us to chew on! Amen!

16 - O LOVE THAT WILT NOT LET ME GO

As I am reading through Job and Psalms, I am struck by how both David and Job understood that God was sovereign...he is in control. At the same time, it's only too clear that God allows us to endure suffering and seemingly, more often than not, doesn't bother to tell us why he permits us to travel such rocky roads. Perhaps a big part of it is simply that we can be an example before others of trusting God even through the hardest times, just as David and Job did. In addition to these well known lives from the Bible, there are many other people who have also suffered greatly through life, frequently not understanding why it is happening in the process. One such person was a Scottish pastor in the 1800s whom we probably know little about: George Matheson. George was an eager student, with a bright future, who managed to graduate from university by the age of 19. However, his eyesight had been deteriorating at the same time, and it gave out altogether while he was still in his teens. Enduring this turn of events just as he planned to study for and enter the ministry was a crushing blow. No less devastating was when his fiancée, more than likely pondering what had happened to him, decided to break off their engagement. But George pressed on. With the sacrificial support of his sister, who learned Hebrew and Greek in order to aid him in his ministry, he did go on to become an effective minister for many years. Some years later, his sister became engaged to be married, and perhaps as a reminder to him of what might have been in his own life, he sunk into a bout of melancholy. Through this dark valley, he was prompted to write the great hymn, "O Love That Wilt Not Let Me Go". We hear some of his pain in the words that Matheson put together: "...my weary soul; my flickering torch; through pain; in dust life's glory..." But all through his life's trials, he cannot shake the persistent, all encompassing love of God, which never leaves him, no matter what his situation. It was the very same lesson that David and Job learned through their own trials.

17 - O GOD, OUR HELP IN AGES PAST

If you ever visit Southampton, down on the lower coast of England, you might be pleasantly surprised to hear a city bell tower ring out the tune of, "O God, our help in ages past", right at the stroke of twelve noon. Written by Isaac Watts, who came from that great city, it has become a notable hymn played at critical national events in Britain, including when Britain declared war at the start of World War 2, as well as at the funeral of Winston Churchill, arguably the greatest Englishman who ever lived. Composed at another crucial moment in British history, when Queen Anne lay dying 300 years ago, without having left an heir, and leaving a lot of uncertainty about the nation's future, it reflects some of the words of Psalm 90. A rather somber statement written by Moses near the end of his life, this psalm reminds us that, just as God has watched over and guided us in the past, so he will do so in the future as well. These same thoughts are expressed in the hymn. And that is not such a bad message for us today as well.

18 - FAIREST LORD JESUS

This hymn, "Fairest Lord Jesus", is one that is very familiar and that I remember hearing and singing for most of my life. But its origin is actually unknown...except for the fact that it is hundreds of years old. In addition to its beautiful words about creation and nature, it alludes to the fact that Jesus is both God and man. The same truth was also pointed out by the early church father, John Chrysosom, the Bishop of Constantinople. This is one of the great mysteries about God, which we will one day in heaven understand more clearly than we do today. Or, as Charles Spurgeon once added in explaining one difference between us and God: "God knows...and we don't!" So, let's hold on to God...even if we don't fully understand him today.

19 - MAN OF SORROWS

One of America's most famous hymn writers was Philip Bliss, who surely would have produced many more songs if his life had not been cut short, along with that of his wife, in a train wreck at the age of 38. Traveling through a snow storm, the train the Blisses was traveling on fell through a collapsed bridge and plunged down a steep ravine. Already, he had produced several hundred hymns by the time he died, including "Man of Sorrows". Bliss was born in a log cabin and grew up on a small country farm in Pennsylvania, later working for several years in lumber camps. His parents were dedicated Christians, and most of the schooling that Philip received was through his own parents' Bible teaching and hymn singing. One day, when Philip was a boy of ten, he was selling his family's vegetables in the nearby town when he heard some beautiful piano music being played for the first time. This grabbed his attention and further opened his awareness to his love for and ability in music. At the age of 11, Philip left home to make his own way, at first toiling as a logger. Later, his singing and composing abilities were discovered and encouraged by others, and he eventually became a music teacher. The hymn,

"Man of Sorrows", presents us with a beautiful picture of how Christ suffered, died, and then rise again to save us. It was published shortly before his tragic death.

20 - JESUS, KEEP ME NEAR THE CROSS

Probably one of my favorite hymn writers was also surely one of the most improbable. Fanny Crosby composed something like 8,500 hymns during her long lifetime. It was not uncommon for her to compose in her head six or seven a day, even thinking over and correcting them in her own mind, since she was practically unable to write except to scratch out her own name. At the same time, she was blind her whole life, and at various times was a destitute recluse. Many people of her day didn't particularly like her hymns, being described as too emotional and sentimental. Yet her words brought our relationship to Christ into a real perspective, as opposed to expressing it in some remote theological idea that was more common among the hymns of the day. The hymn, "Jesus, keep me near the cross", brings the reality of what Christ accomplished by his death on the cross into clear and understandable perspective. Crosby uses remarkably descriptive terms to show us the power and greatness and reality of what Jesus did for us, to show us why the cross was so important. In spite of being ridiculed at times, of being blind, and even destitute, Miss Crosby became a household name in the 1800s, as D.L. Moody used many of her hymns in his crusades and promoted her work. She met several Presidents, became a teacher of the blind, was considered the queen of Gospel songwriters, and was the most prolific of all American hymn composers in the nineteenth century. When Moody asked her, according to legend, what her one wish would be, he expected her to want her sight. Instead she replied: "I wish to remain blind for the rest of my life. For I hope to see the face of Jesus before I see anyone else's!" What a remarkable lady!

21 - WHEN PEACE LIKE A RIVER

I always enjoy reading how various writers are inspired by some particular experience to then write a wonderful hymn. Perhaps none was more tragic than the events that inspired Horatio Spafford to compose the words to the beautiful hymn, "When Peace Like a River." Spafford was a successful lawyer, a friend of D.L. Moody, whose investments and assets were largely wiped out by the great Chicago fire. His only son also died from scarlet fever. Wanting to have some time away and to regroup, he decided to take his wife and four young daughters on an extended trip to Europe, where he also planned to assist Moody with one of his preaching tours. They booked a ship voyage across the Atlantic...but at the last minute, Spafford was delayed by urgent business. He decided to send his family on ahead of himself and planned to rejoin them as quickly as he could. His wife and four girls set sail...but several days later he received a rather terse telegram from his wife: "Only I survived." The ship had collided with another vessel in the middle of the ocean, which thus sent the ship and most of its passengers to the bottom of the sea. Somehow his wife was saved. Utterly devastated, Spafford nevertheless headed out on another ship shortly afterwards to meet his wife. As his ship sailed toward the middle of the Atlantic, the captain told Spafford, "This is right about where their ship went down." What an overwhelming feeling must have coursed through his body at that moment, thinking that his dearly loved young daughters were right then a mile or so beneath him. Rather than being completely crushed, or perhaps in spite of it, Spafford returned to his cabin and penned these lovely, lovely words. I don't know if he ever fully recovered from his losses...but at that moment, at least, he knew that God was in control, and that the Almighty held him close.

22 - MY HOPE IS BUILT ON NOTHING LESS

A remarkable story of grace and redemption is that of Edward Mote, who lived in England in the 1800s. Owners of a pub in London, his parents frequently left him to his own devices on the streets of the city. Edward later reflected, "I grew up knowing nothing at all about God." In his teens, he was trained as a cabinetmaker, a profession he pursued well into his 50s. In addition to teaching Mote his trade, his master teacher also led him to the Lord. After that he become a Baptist preacher. At one point, his congregation wanted to thank and bless him...and they offered him the ownership of the church building. "I do not want the building," he replied. "I only want the pulpit. And if I ever cease preaching Christ, then you need to drive me out of it!" Continuing to preach every Sunday until shortly before he passed away in his 70s, Mote also wrote hymns, at one point publishing a book with nearly 100 of his hymns. Recognizing his own rescue from an empty and unstable life, he composed the well known and well loved hymn, "My Hope is Built on Nothing Less".

23 - BECAUSE HE LIVES

Lindsay Terry has shared the beautiful story behind a more contemporary song than the "traditional hymns" from previous generations. Here it is:

"When Gloria Sickal and Bill Gaither were single and teaching in Alexandria, Indiana, they met and began to share ideas about songs. Gloria, the English major in college, would in later years become the predominant writer of the lyrics in their songs, while Bill's forte would be the musical settings. Their joint efforts, which began in that Alexandria high school, blossomed into a prolific husband and wife songwriting duo. Bill, in most of their songwriting ventures, will write a musical setting with an idea in mind and Gloria, using the same idea, will write the lyrics. To date, they have written more than 700 songs, produced 60 recordings and several musicals. In the late 1960s, while expecting their third child, the Gaithers were going through a rather traumatic time in their lives. Bill was recovering from a bout with mononucleosis. It was a special period of anxiety and mental anguish for Gloria. The thought of bringing another child into this world, with all of the 'craziness', was taking its toll on her.

On New Year's Eve, she was sitting in their living room, in agony and fear. The educational system was being infiltrated with the 'God is dead' idea, while drug abuse and racial tensions were increasing. Then suddenly, and quite unexpectedly, she was filled with a gentle, calming peace. It was as if her heavenly Father, like an attentive mother bending over her baby, saw his child and came to her rescue. The panic gave way to calmness and an assurance that only the Lord can impart. She was assured that the future would be just fine, left in God's hands.

Shortly after the baby was born, both Bill and Gloria remembered that the power of the blessed Holy Spirit seemed to come to their aid. Christ's resurrection, in all of its power and affirmation in their lives, revitalized their thinking. To Gloria, it was life conquering death in their daily activities. Joy once again dominated the fearful circumstances of the day. Those events gave rise to one of the most famous Christian songs of our time, 'Because He Lives'. In this song, which begins, 'God sent His son, they called Him Jesus', we are reminded that Christ came to this earth. And the purpose for His coming was that we might be able to face tomorrow, with all of the uncertainty that it brings. She also reminds us that God holds the future right in his hands and makes life worth living for all who trust in him."

"Because I live, you also will live."

John 14:19 NIV

24 - PRAISE TO THE LORD, THE ALMIGHTY

I don't suppose many folks who live to be only 30 become world famous in that short span of life. Joachim Neander, however, did just that. Wasting away of tuberculosis just as he turned 30, Joachim lived in a corner of Germany named for his own family, the Neander Valley. It was here, nearly 200 years after his death, that a skull was discovered, which led to the idea of the "Neanderthal man", named for this very same Calvinist pastor, schoolmaster, and hymn writer. Before he passed away, Neander had composed some 60 hymns, one being the still well-known, "Praise to the Lord, the Almighty". Although growing up living a rather loose and immoral life, Joachim was dramatically converted at a young age as he attended a service by a visiting preacher. Serving as a schoolmaster for some time, Joachim nevertheless ran into trouble by attaching himself to the Pietists, whose focus on individual spirituality ran counter to the traditions of the established Lutheran Church. Dismissed from his post, Joachim lived part of his life in seclusion in the Neander Valley. Then, declining health cut short his life. In spite of these difficulties, Joachim's hymns are filled with joy and praise and have blessed many down through the centuries.

25 - THE GOD OF ABRAHAM PRAISE

Thomas Olivers was a scoundrel. Born in Wales 300 years ago, his parents both died when he was a child. He trained to become a shoemaker but at the same time began living loose and recklessly. Following a scandal, he had to leave town, and he wandered over into England. Landing in Bristol, he stumbled upon a meeting with the Great Awakening preacher, George Whitefield, who was preaching from Zechariah 3:2, "...a brand plucked from the fire..." Olivers recognized himself in those words and was converted then and there. Entering the ministry himself, he became a powerful preacher, serving with John Wesley. At the same time, Thomas developed and enjoyed good relations with Jewish leaders of the day. At one of their meetings, he was captivated by some of their music and went on to develop it into the well loved Christian hymn, "The God of Abraham Praise", which has been a blessing to many down through the ages. We may never fully understand how God will choose to use us in this life, but the story of Thomas Olivers is a reminder that God's Word is powerful, and it speaks to and changes the hearts of the most unlikely of people.

26 - MY FAITH LOOKS UP TO THEE

In his early 20s, Ray Palmer wanted to enter the ministry. But at his young age, he already felt exhausted and burned out. Working at a dry goods shop, studying at Yale, and teaching at a girls' school, what he really wanted to do was to become a minister. But his schedule left him drained and depressed. One day, he chanced upon a friend, Lowell Mason, who was a musician and hymn writer. On a lark, Mason asked his friend, Ray, if he wanted to contribute something toward a hymnal that Mason was putting together. Not having intended it for public consumption, Palmer sometime earlier, in a moment of despair, had composed the words of "My Faith Looks up to Thee". Showing these words to Mason somewhat apologetically, Palmer was surprised to hear these words coming from his friend: "Ray, you may do many different things in your life. But I dare say that you will one day be best remembered for these very words in your hymn, "My Faith Looks up to Thee". Mason knew talent and inspiration when he saw it...and his prophesy turned out to be true. Though Palmer went on to enter the ministry and wrote hymns as well, he will always be associated with his first hymn, written at a very low and lonely point in his life.

27 - JESUS THE VERY THOUGHT OF THEE

Nearly 1,000 years ago, a boy was born in the wine country of France. He was given the name Bernard (pronounced somewhat like Bare-nar in French). Born in a castle to a well to do family, and with a father who participated as a knight in the first Crusade, Bernard chose to pursue an unlikely path. Being a rather thoughtful fellow, and encouraged by the spirituality of his mother in particular, Bernard decided to become a monk and moved into a monastery. Later, he was asked to open a daughter monastery in Clairvaux, and thus the name he became known to the world by. He went on to counsel popes and even to preach to the king of France. One of the monks under his care would later become a pope himself, Pope Eugene III. But most of all, Bernard was captivated with knowing God, learning of his grace toward us, and serving the needy. That was his true passion throughout his life. During his lifetime, Bernard wrote many sermons and letters, and the hymn, "Jesus, the very thought of thee", is generally attributed to him.

28 - JESUS, PRICELESS TREASURE

Johann Franck was born in Germany in a rather unfortunate year, 1618. It marked the start of the 30 Years War, a conflict that devastated much of Europe and shifted the balance of power between the nations. While probably less that 500,000 soldiers died during the various conflicts, perhaps as many as 5 million civilians died, largely from bubonic plague, starvation, or other illnesses. The population of Europe was so badly decimated that it was only 100 years later that the overall population recovered to prewar levels. This was the landscape that Franck was born into. A lawyer, poet, and hymn writer, Franck wrote at a time which in some ways matches what we face today, with war, turmoil, starvation, and pandemic spread around the world. It no doubt seemed like a time devoid of any hope. But Johann Franck understood where our true hope lies, in Jesus, and so this is what he wrote about in the hymn, "Jesus, priceless treasure", one of the more than 100 hymns he wrote during his lifetime, which was produced a few years after the war ended. It contains clear references to our hope and security being in Jesus, and was written during that time when no doubt many may have wondered what

hope was left in the world.
Hence, all earthly treasure!
Jesus is my pleasure;
Jesus is my choice.
Hence, all empty glory!
What to me thy story
Told with tempting voice?
Pain or loss or shame or cross
Shall not from my Savior move me,
Since He chose to love me.

29 - CROWN HIM WITH MANY CROWNS

Though he was born in England, Matthew Bridges lived a number of his years in Canada and then returned to England before his death. Raised in the Anglican Church, Bridges was part of a group, popular at the time, that sought to go back to the early church to investigate their traditions, liturgy, and ways of worship. In doing so, many of the folks in this movement switched allegiances to the Roman Catholic Church. Bridges himself was first a minister in the Anglican Church and then later became a priest in the Catholic Church. He wrote a number of hymns, and this one, which in his lyrics referred to the Virgin Mary, became accepted by Protestant churches after it was rewritten without the references to Mary. Bridges' hymn identifies Jesus Christ as the King of kings and Lord of lords, and perhaps was in part motivated by the reference in Revelation 5:13 to the Lamb on the throne, as well as Revelation 19:12 which speaks of many crowns.

30 - GOD MOVES IN A MYSTERIOUS WAY

Living at the same time as the United States was becoming a nation, William Cowper, in England, was a tortured soul on several fronts. All five of William's older siblings died in infancy. Then, when he was six, his mother passed away while giving birth to his younger brother, John. He was teased and taunted at school. His father vetoed his choice of a bride. And his father forced him to study law, which was not really what he wanted to do. When he learned that he would have to pass his Bar before the House of Lords in Parliament, it sent him into a depressed downward spiral. Later, struggling with ongoing depression, Cowper was confined to an insane asylum. One day William was strolling in the asylum's garden and noticed a Bible that someone had left on a bench (something that I greatly enjoy doing as well!). Picking up God's Book, he opened it and began to read of Christ's atoning work on his behalf. This discovery led to his surrendering himself to God. Cowper was well known across Britain for his poetry... and for his hymn writing...and even in these, his agony is revealed. Perhaps his best known hymn, "God Moves in a Mysterious Way", also hints at his struggles to cope with life. For example, in this hymn, he says: "Ye fearful saints, fresh courage take; the clouds ye so much dread are big with mercy...". It's almost as if he was talking to and trying to convince himself of this very truth. Cowper was also good buddies with "Amazing Grace" hymn writer, John Newton, who strived on occasion to prevent William from ending his life. Together they partnered to produce a volume of their own hymns. The deep struggles and travails of these tarnished and defective men have been a great blessing to us who follow as they wrote down their thoughts and prayers to God...

31 - JESUS SHALL REIGN WHERE E'ER THE SUN

Considered the father of modern English hymns and honored for his life in Westminster Abbey, Isaac Watts, poet, pastor, and hymn writer, in 1719, put together a paraphrase of the book of the Psalms, which included the hymn, "Jesus Shall Reign", based on Psalm 72. The hymn focuses on missionary effort and endeavor, and Watts envisioned a time when Christ would be acknowledged and worshiped all across the globe, which, up to that point, was only a very novel idea. William Carey, the father of modern missions, was still decades away from heading off to India. Olympic runner Eric Liddell sang stanzas of the hymn as he set sail from Scotland to head out for missionary service in China. Thousands of former cannibals in the South Sea Islands also gathered in 1862 to celebrate their rescue from savagery to Christianity, and they sung this same hymn. Still today, 300 years after being composed, it remains very pertinent and popular.

32 - THE CHURCH'S ONE FOUNDATION

Concerned about a drift away from Biblical theology in nineteenth century South Africa, with one Anglican Bishop even questioning the Bible's authenticity, Samuel Stone set out to compose a series of hymns on the Apostles' Creed, including "The Church's One Foundation", as the controversy had begun to spill over into Britain as well. Studying at Oxford University, Samuel earlier had won a competition in English composition. Later, he became a priest in the Anglican Church in Oxford. Liberal theology was beginning to take hold, and Samuel Stone desired to make a clear statement in defense of the traditional authority of the Scriptures as God's Holy Word. Using different themes from the Creed, Stone put together 12 hymns, of which this is perhaps the most important. His desire was to encourage the church to hold firmly to the fundamental truths of the faith during times of controversy and change.

33 - WHILE SHEPHERDS WATCHED THEIR FLOCKS BY NIGHT

If someone presented us with "A New Version of the Psalms of David", would it cause us to raise our eyebrows a bit, as we wondered what new ideas someone might be adding to Scripture? That is exactly what happened over 300 years ago, when, in 1696, Nahum Tate produced a new and improved version of the Psalter that was being sung by the Church of England at the time (and composed over 100 years earlier in the 1500s). Included in the Psalter was this hymn, which became the first to be accepted from outside the Psalms, being a close account of the Christmas story from Luke 2. After some initial skepticism and complaints, the new hymns presented my Tate were accepted and became the standard sung in the Anglican Church for over 200 years...and of course this hymn continues to be well appreciated all across the world. Born in Ireland, Nahum Tate moved to England and eventually rose to become a Poet Laureate in the nation. His hymn presents the

events surrounding the birth of our Savior Jesus
Christ.

34 - HARK! THE HERALD ANGELS SING

Shortly after his conversion to Christianity, Charles Wesley began to put what he was learning about the Gospel into song. His brother, John, stated that Charles' hymns were filled with wonderful theology, which they certainly are. Charles wanted to convey the truths of the Gospel in his songs so that those who were not privileged or well educated could hear the Message of God's love. As he was walking to church one Christmas day, he was inspired by the church bells ringing all across London, and the words of this hymn began to form in his mind. At first written as a poem to be read on Christmas, the composition later was put to music as the hymn we now know, with the assistance of George Whitefield. The hymn proclaims the Good News of Christ coming to reconcile the sinner back to God. Describing Christ using a number of the names that reveal his nature, Wesley gave an explanation of why Christ came and what he accomplished through his life, death, and resurrection.

35 - JOY TO THE WORLD, THE LORD IS COME

Since being initially composed some 300 years ago by Isaac Watts, "Joy to the World" has become perhaps the most popular and well known hymn for Christmas. Interestingly, though, when Watts first wrote it up, it was part of a book of hymns based on the Psalms, this one being drawn from verses in Psalms 96 & 98. Watts wrote to demonstrate how the Psalms brought out and represented the coming of Christ, and this hymn also does the same, pointing to his coming to earth and what he accomplished in conquering sin. Watts was considered radical in his day as he shook up the status quo in how the church generally depicted Scripture and worship, and many people did not appreciate him at the time. In this wonderful hymn, though, he joins Christ's coming at Christmas with his work on our behalf as well as his return to make all things right.

36 - GLORIOUS THINGS OF THEE ARE SPOKEN

One of the great hymns that the slave trader turned preacher, John Newton, composed (and published along with his buddy, William Cowper) was "Glorious Things of Thee are Spoken". It speaks of the great names of God, of the people of God purchased with Christ's own blood, and of heaven as being God's dwelling place, of being in God's presence. It was put to a musical tune by Franz Josef Haydn, the famous Austrian composer. Haydn had written the music in celebration of the Emperor of Austria, and it was used in conjunction with Austria's national anthem. Later it was also adapted as the tune for the German national anthem. The hymn that Newton wrote remains, hundreds of years later, one of the great songs of worship in the church.

37 - FOR ALL THE SAINTS

Quite often, when I am wrestling with a spiritual issue...or just trying to get through life...I am reminded of, and thankful for, those who have gone before us. Those who also have wrestled and struggled through life, and who have made it to the finish life. I am thankful for their courage, their persistence, their example. That, really, is what this hymn, "For all the Saints", is celebrating as well. Reflecting on those who are listed in Hebrews 11 in particular, the hymn reminds us of our fellowship and communion with these folks who have gone before us. And really, scattered all across the Bible, we see examples of the same... those who have toiled and battled and preceded us. Thank God for them, thank the Lord for including their stories and their wobbly tales for our encouragement as well. And I am thankful for the Oxford educated Anglican Bishop William How, who put this hymn together. Pastor How lived and toiled among the least and the lowest, miners and laborers in the slums of London and elsewhere, and he, too, was grateful for those who went before us.

38 - WHAT A FRIEND WE HAVE IN JESUS

Joseph Scriven endured tragedy upon tragedy in his troubled life. Just as he was hoping to be married, his fiancée in Ireland fell from her horse while crossing a bridge, and drowned in a lake on the day before their wedding was planned, nearly 200 years ago. Scriven, waiting on the other side of the bridge, watched this all unfold. In his utter grief, the young man decided to quit Dublin and leave for Canada, packed his bags, and left his mother behind. Following a time of pastoring and teaching, he threw himself into obscure charity work...chopping firewood for widows, giving away his clothing to those more needy, and spreading his money to those without. Some years later, Joseph received word that his mother was enduring her own health crisis. The young man gathered his creative skills and wrote a poem which became known eventually as, "What a friend we have in Jesus". This he did for his mother alone, never intending anyone else to see it. But his sneaky mother passed it on to a friend...who published it as a hymn, though at the time no one knew the author. At about the same time, Joseph again fell in love and planned his wedding. And once again, tragedy visited Scriven. His fiancée contracted tuberculosis...and soon passed away. Joseph continued to bury himself in his charitable endeavors. Much later, not long before his own death, Scriven lay in bed as a friend came to comfort him. The friend spied, next to Scriven's bed, the scribbled poem, "What a Friend we have in Jesus", that he now asked his weak friend about. Joseph acknowledged what no one knew up to that moment...he was the one who had composed that poem years earlier for his own mother during a time of testing in her life. His friend asked him, "Is it true that you wrote this text?" "The Lord and I did it together, he said." All my life, I've been blessed by this hymn as well, a gift to us, born out of the excruciating pain of another.

39 - THE KING OF LOVE MY SHEPHERD IS

Digging into the lives of some of the familiar hymn writers can uncover some interesting details. Henry Williams Baker was an Anglican pastor who served in a small rural community of less than 200 people, just next to Wales, in England. His father was a decorated naval officer who had fought with distinction against the Americans in the War of 1812 (but we won't hold that against him!). As Henry settled into this quiet neighborhood, he pulled out his pen and came up with some well known hymns. This particular one, "The King of love my Shepherd is", is interesting in that it combines the idea of the Lord as our shepherd in Psalm 23 with the Good Shepherd that Jesus identified himself with in John 10. That is also the passage included on my little brother's grave stone. After graduating from Cambridge University, Baker, aged 30, took up his pastorate in this little community where he became greatly loved. He opened the first village schoolhouse, and the early building still exists today. After one unsuccessful test of the waters, Baker decided to remain unmarried, and instead served the people of his parish until his death at age 55. One of his main accomplishments was contributing to the publication of "Hymns Ancient & Modern", which, unusual for that day, combines texts and tunes on the same page, so that anyone could sing the music more easily. And, as he lay dying, Baker repeated some of the words of this hymn, according to his good friend who was with him at that moment. It was also sung at the funeral of Princess Diana in 1997.

40 - MAY THE MIND OF CHRIST, MY SAVIOR

Some hymns are composed out of dramatic or challenging situations. Others are composed by famous writers who have written hundreds or even thousands of hymns, many of them well known. Then there are some odd ones which seem to have appeared out of nowhere, written by no one special, for no apparent obvious reason. Such is perhaps the case of, "May the Mind of Christ my Savior". Written by Kate Barclay Wilkinson, it was not published until shortly before her death, a dozen or more years after it was written. We know almost nothing about Mrs. Wilkinson, except that she may have worked with young women in London, and she may have been involved with the Keswick Convention in the UK. And that is about all we know. But the hymn is actually rather profound and deep, speaking of how we should walk as Christians. It has been suggested that the six stanzas of the hymn were for each day of the week, leading up to the Lord's Day, though of course they carry truths which we need to heed and be mindful of each and every day. The first stanza speaks of having the mind of Christ, taken from Philippians 2. Following that, we are told to include in our lives God's Word (Colossians 3), his peace, and his love, and to live our lives with our attention on Jesus (Hebrews 12), and finally, to demonstrate the beauty of Christ in our lives. The fact that God can use a lone hymn, written by an unknown person, to be a blessing to so many people in the generations that follow is actually a wonderful encouragement and comfort to us, as we travel through life, perhaps at times pondering whether our efforts will have much value for eternity. It is God who uses and multiplies what we have to offer him.

41 - COME, WE THAT LOVE THE LORD

Following his common practice, British hymn writer Isaac Watts composed this hymn into a devotional style. John Wesley greatly appreciated the words and included it in his "Psalms and Hymns, 'Charlestown' Collection", which became the first hymnal published in the American colonies when Wesley visited on a missionary journey in the early 1700s, before the American Revolution. In addition to speaking of worship here on earth, the words point us to heaven and the future we have to look forward to one day. Especially during these times of turmoil in our world today, this is a comforting song which lifts our focus and attention to heaven and eternal things.

42 - HOW FIRM A FOUNDATION

Although no one seems to know for sure who authored this hymn, it has been a favorite of many for over 200 years. Sung by both armies during the US Civil War, it was also sung by the troops during the Spanish-American War. And it was a favorite of Andrew Jackson, Teddy Roosevelt, and Robert E. Lee, being played at each of their funerals. Full of references to numerous Scripture passages, it continues to bless us to this day and reminds us that we can trust in God during turbulent and difficult times.

43 - JUST AS I AM

This very familiar hymn has a beautiful story attached to it...something perhaps you and I need to remind each other of. Two hundred years ago, Charlotte Elliot was a gifted artist and writer in England. But a serious illness knocked her off her feet, and she became crippled and depressed, spending the following decades feeling useless to anyone and wrestling with her pain and despondency. Sometime along the way, a pastor friend from Switzerland paid her a visit to encourage her. She brushed him off...then later felt guilty about it. Deciding she needed to get her spiritual house in order, she went to apologize to the pastor. She confessed that she wanted to get herself right with God but had too much rubble in her life to clean up first. The wise man then told her, "Just come as you are." Those words stayed with her, and more than a decade later she remembered them and came up with this simple but powerful hymn of trusting Jesus and finding forgiveness in him.

44 - JESUS, THY BLOOD AND RIGHTEOUSNESS

Along with about 2,000 others, Nicolaus von Zinzendorf wrote this hymn nearly 200 years ago. Although we are familiar with only a few of its stanzas, his original hymn contained 33! It was then translated into English by John Wesley (who apparently picked up German along with all his preaching and horseback riding). It contains a wonderful explanation of how Christ's death and righteousness were completely sufficient to save us from our sinful nature. Zinzendorf was strongly influenced by his pious grandmother and his teachers, who conveyed to him the importance of reaching a lost world with the saving truth of the Gospel. As a legal councilor, he purchased a large estate which he used to shelter religious refugees. Many of these were Moravians, committed...and persecuted...believers who traced their roots back to the reformer John Hus in the 1400s. Zinzendorf eventually housed about 300 of these Moravian refugees, establishing a community of them at his estate. Later, this community published its own book of nearly 1,000 hymns, including over 200 authored by Nicolaus. All of them communicated holiness and a zeal for missions. Nicolaus Ludwig Graf von Zinzendorf was remarkable in that he came from wealthy nobility, yet he was powerfully influenced by the work of Christ on our behalf... and the life we should live in response to what Christ did for us. Eventually resigning his legal responsibilities, he spent his life serving the Moravians and preaching Christ and him crucified, traveling all across Europe and even to North America. On one occasion, he visited the Düsseldorf art gallery and stood before a painting of Jesus wearing a crown of bloody thorns. Written below the art were these words: "All this I have done for Thee; What doest thou for me?" Forever afterwards his motto was, "I have but one passion, and that is He, and only He."

45 - HOW SWEET THE NAME OF JESUS SOUNDS

Because of my love of and curiosity about history, it's interesting to speculate sometimes about what people were thinking of or wrestling with during some monumental historical events. Take this hymn, for example. Penned by the notorious former slave trader, John Newton, it has blessed countless people on both sides of the Atlantic and even further afield. But interestingly, he wrote the hymn during the American Revolution, when the colonies and Britain were in mortal combat. Yet, folks on both sides were greatly blessed by the words, perhaps even both singing it as they fired at each other. The wonderful words of this poem remind us of who Jesus is for us, how he restores, heals, and cares for us, telling us to turn to him during our journey through life, with its many ups and downs. Newton would often try to come up with simple words that could be sung which were tied in with his sermon messages and which would help the ordinary folks in his congregation take to heart the message he was trying to convey to them. The first phrase would have been especially meaningful to Newton, who, as a young slave trader, lived...and lived among men who experienced...the most foul mouthed existence possible, regularly takes the Lord's name in vain. Interestingly, Newton connected the hymn to "Solomon's Song", and noted Song of Solomon 1:3 along side it. This verse alludes to the sweet fragrance of a name, and in Newton's case, especially after the rough life he had lived, refers to the beauty of the name of Jesus, who saved and redeemed him out of his lost existence.

46 - O, FOR A THOUSAND TONGUES TO SING

The youngest of 18 children, Charles Wesley certainly rose in prominence to make a name for himself. He became an itinerant preacher in England, worked in reaching out to prisoners, and apparently in his spare time, wrote over 6,000 hymns, many of the greatest and most familiar that we know and still sing. He and his well known brother John would comment that they had more conversions through these hymns than through their preaching!

"O for a Thousand Tongues to Sing" was specially written by him in 1739 to celebrate the first anniversary of his conversion or reaffirmation of his faith. Wesley wanted to celebrate each of his spiritual birthdays by writing a hymn of praise to God, and this one was most often placed at the beginning of the Methodist hymnals (and it still is right at the front of my own Methodist hymnal...). Wesley apparently came up with the phrase used in the title of this hymn from his friend Peter Boehler, who was a Moravian teacher and who said to Wesley, "Had I a thousand tongues, I would praise God with them all." Also, the text of this hymn includes his own spiritual experience. When he had been seriously ill in bed, his brother and some friends visited him and sang a hymn. After they left, one beautiful phrase struck him in his heart, which has been woven into another verse of the hymn: "Jesus! The name that charms our fears that bids our sorrows cease." Beautiful and comforting words indeed!

47 - JESUS, SAVIOR, PILOT ME

Following pastorates in other churches, in 1870, Edward Hopper became the pastor of a small church in New York harbor known as the Church of Sea and Land. Hopper's father was a merchant in the area, and his mother was descended from persecuted French Huguenots. As perhaps can he imagined, a good number of the folks who attended the church were sailors who passed through the harbor. Hopper enjoyed getting to know the sailors traveling through New York from all over the world and sought to minister to their needs. Using language they could understand and relate to, Hopper composed this hymn especially for them, but also for anyone seeking to find their way through life. Sometimes known as the "Sailor's Hymn", it was not his only hymn, but it is the one we remember the best. The theme of his text comes from Matthew 8:23-27, where we read how Jesus calmed the raging Sea of Galilee.

Major D. W. Whittle told the following incident in connection with this hymn: "I went with General Howard to hold meetings for the soldiers at Tampa, Florida, and one day while going through the camp I found a young man dying of fever. I knelt by his side and asked him if he was a

Christian. He replied that he was not, but he asked me to pray for him. I did so, though he did not give his heart to Jesus at that time. I went away with a sorrowing heart and promised to return another day. Two days later I visited him again and, praying with him once more, the Lord put into my mind to sing, 'Jesus, Saviour, pilot me'. The dying soldier said: 'Oh, that sounds good; it puts me in mind of my beloved sister in Michigan, who used to sing this hymn for me before I entered the army.' He wanted me to repeat it over and over again for him, and finally he asked: 'Will Jesus be my pilot into the haven of rest?' I told the young man that Jesus would. 'Then', he said, 'I will trust him with all my heart.' The next day I called to see him again, but his comrade said: 'He passed away during the night.'"

48 - JESUS, LOVER OF MY SOUL

There are a number of intriguing stories that suggest what might have prompted Charles Wesley to write the hymn, "Jesus, lover of my soul". But it seems that no one really knows the circumstances under which he wrote it. Apparently written at about age 30, not long after Wesley had truly embraced Christianity for himself, it became one of the greatest and most loved of all the thousands of his hymns, and it is especially known for the manner in which it expresses Jesus' love for us. Christ not only is full of love for us, he also saves us during turbulent times, and even more, his grace is exceedingly abundant enough to cover and deal with all our sins. That just about covers all our needs! One story about the hymn's origin includes a bird that flew into Wesley's room for safety during a rainstorm, another about an incident where Charles hid under a hedge with his brother after being attacked by an angry mob opposed to their preaching in Ireland. However, it does perhaps reflect three significant experiences in his early life: the near sinking of his ship during a storm on the ocean when returning to England from ministering in the colony of Georgia in 1736; his great spiritual awakening and change in 1738; and his ministry to inmates in prison. Wesley praises Jesus throughout this hymn as a source of refuge, guidance, and salvation in times of uncertainty and grief. This classic hymn describes the intimacy that Jesus offers us in our relationship with Him. At its core, Christianity is about having a personal and intimate relationship with our Savior Jesus, not about a series of rules or about our striving to somehow reach God. One interesting story associated with the hymn is as follows: Decades after the war, at a gathering of veterans of the Civil War, a former Confederate recalled that late one evening during the war, he was on patrol and came upon a Yankee sentry. He aimed his gun with a clear shot, and just as he was ready to pull the trigger, the sentry broke into singing, "Jesus, lover of my soul, let me to thy bosom fly..." The gunman froze and listened. As the Union guard continued to sing, "Cover my defenseless head with the shadow of thy wing", the soldier lowered his gun and crept away. "I couldn't kill that man though he were 10 times my enemy," he recalled. Then a Union veteran spoke up, "Was that in the battle of Atlanta in 1864?" Indeed, it was. "I was that sentry!" the Union veteran exclaimed. He spoke of his fear of battle, the sense of hopelessness he felt that night on patrol, and the peace and comfort brought by singing the hymn. Remarkable how God uses things we offer, such as this hymn, in situations we could never envision!

49 - GUIDE ME, O THOU GREAT JEHOVAH

During the early 1700s, the ideas from the enlightenment and rationalism were taking root across Europe and Britain, and spilling over into the American colonies. Part of the resulting consequences was a decline in religious commitment. Thankfully, at just about the same time, a number of zealous and passionate preachers appeared on the scene and were instrumental in bringing about what became known as the Great Awakening. Preachers such as George Whitefield, the Wesley brothers, and Jonathan Edwards helped to rekindle a renewal and commitment to a personal relationship with God and to the church. As these events were taking place, a young man in Wales, in Britain, heard a sermon preached in a church cemetery. The message had such an impact on him that he turned from pursuing medicine to becoming an itinerant preacher himself. During the next 40+ years, William Williams accomplished in his home country of Wales what was also taking place in those other areas. Traveling on horseback, Williams preached...and sang...his way to great crowds across the land. Along with the great English hymn writers, Williams composed about 800 hymns, the best remembered being, "Guide me, O thou great Jehovah". The song compares our Christian life and walk to the wanderings of the children of Israel. It became a favorite in Wales, even being considered as something of an unofficial national anthem. During World War 1, Welch soldiers in the trenches would at times sing the hymn, and opposing German soldiers would on occasion pick up the singing as well. The hymn was sung at Queen Elizabeth's Diamond Jubilee Celebration, Princess Diana's funeral, and the wedding of Prince William to Katherine Middleton. As President James Garfield lay dying, his wife also comforted him as she sang the words to him.

50 - JESUS CALLS US, O'ER THE TUMULT

As a little girl, Cecil Frances Alexander discovered great pleasure in scribbling down her thoughts. However, as her father was a rather strict Anglican priest (who eventually became the head of the church in Ireland), she hid her writings where her father would not find them, knowing he would probably disapprove. One day, though, he did uncover some of her work, stuffed under a rug. As he looked through it, he was impressed by what she had done. So he actually encouraged her to continue with her writing. Eventually, she took to writing poems and hymns for children, composing several hundred hymns for a young audience. She was particularly concerned about the good training that children should receive at a young age. Interestingly, though, her best remembered hymn ("Jesus calls us o'er the tumult") was for adults, written at the request of her husband for his church members as he prepared a sermon on Jesus calling his disciples. Mrs. Alexander also showed her concern for disadvantaged people by traveling many miles regularly to visit the sick and the poor, and providing food, warm clothes, and medical supplies as the nation was recovering after the potato famines of the mid-1800s. She and her sister also founded a school for the deaf. She willingly gave away the money she made from her hymn and poetry collections, funded the school for deaf children, and supported women who got into trouble. A simple women...who used what she had to make a profound impact.

51 - A MIGHTY FORTRESS IS OUR GOD

Martin Luther is one of the best known names in Protestantism, having opposed certain practices in the Catholic Church; having had the courage to stand up against the establishment and suffering for years as a result of it, even having his life threatened; starting a branch of the church that was important in those early days of the Reformation; translating the Bible into German, which made it accessible to the common people... and even writing a few hymns on the side. Luther came to discover through his Bible reading that true Christianity did not depend upon what we know about God, but upon a right personal relationship with God. God's forgiveness through the sacrificial death of Christ became all important to Luther. Coming from an area of Germany known for its music, Luther was part of a boys' choir in his youth, and so became trained in music. As an adult, he worked to renew congregational singing and to being hymnals into the churches. By far and away the best known hymn he wrote, and which also defined the Reformation, was "A Mighty Fortress is our God". Inspired by Psalm

46 ("God is our refuge and strength."), Luther's hymn gave him courage during his greatest trials and was no doubt an encouragement even to his contemporaries who also dared to stand up in protest of the traditions of the established church.

52 - COME, THOU ALMIGHTY KING

The words in the hymn, "Come, Thou Almighty King", sound like commands to the Sovereign God to prove himself, interspersed with praise to the Almighty. There's a command in almost every line. The song makes one think of a battle psalm of David, a warrior's cry to the Lord, an urgent appeal for God's vengeance to come. The song's composer is anonymous, but the words in it give us a hint of the songwriter's situation, who he might have been, and of his abiding faith in God. Some folks believe Charles Wesley composed the words, since its call to God for protection from enemies is a familiar theme in his songs. It first appeared in 1757 along with a message by Charles' brother, John. The Wesleys suffered persecution for their beliefs, so the song's message matches what they might have been pouring out of their souls, like what King David expressed in his psalms while on the run from his enemies. The song's arrival nearly coincided with a well-known tune, "God Save Our Gracious King", which was in honor of England's royalty, but which didn't go down well with Methodists. Instead, they latched onto "Come Thou Almighty King", which was sung to the same music, but sung to an entirely different king.

During the American Revolutionary War, a group of British soldiers attended a church service in New York. They demanded that the congregation sing "God Save Our Gracious King" for the king of England. The congregation did sing the tune, but the words they used were from "Come, Thou Almighty King". The song was also composed to remind Christians of the Trinity. Verse 1 is to the Father; verse 2 recognizes the Incarnate Word, the Father's Son; the following two verses refer to the Spirit as our Comforter; and finally, there is a reference to the three in one, the Trinity. Did Charles Wesley in fact write the hymn? Most likely he wouldn't want us to debate it for long. He'd want us to think about the message of the song. God is called upon with requests for 25 things in these five verses (actually the last four are reminders of what we as worshippers do, with his help). It might make one wonder, "Does he grow weary of my neediness?" If nothing else, the song reminds me that God exists to hear my constant cries, to be my Savior in all things.

53 - WHEN I SURVEY THE WONDROUS CROSS

Englishman Isaac Watts wrote "When I Survey the Wondrous Cross." This hymn focuses on the purpose of Jesus' death and its significance for a Christian. At the time of Watt's birth in 1674, English churches sang only metrical psalms. Over his lifetime, Watts introduced modern hymn singing by producing 600 hymns published in several collections and used widely in churches in England and colonial America. This hymn has often been called the greatest hymn in the English language. A contemporary of Isaac Watts said of it, "There may be a few others equally great, but there is none greater." The hymn writer, Charles Wesley said, "I would rather have written that one hymn than all of my own." The song was intended as a communion hymn and is headed with a reference to Paul's letter to the Galatians: "Crucifixion to the world by the cross of Christ". Isaac describes the cross as the meeting place of love and sorrow - suffering and salvation. The cross is the intersection where God forgave his children by paying for the punishment they deserved. But the words also serve to highlight the wonder and amazement that should be ours as we think about the cross. That the sinless Son of God was willing to die in order to break the power of this wicked world over the human soul — should cause profound wonder and awe at the love of Christ and of the one who sent him into this world to save sinners. Watts explained: "Where the Psalmist describes religion by the fear of God, I have often joined faith and love to it. Where he speaks of the pardon of sin through the mercies of God, I rather choose to mention the sacrifice of Christ, the Lamb of God. Where He promises abundance of wealth, honor, and long life, I have changed some of these typical blessings for grace, glory, and life eternal, which are brought to light by the Gospel, and promised in the New Testament."

54 - ALL GLORY, LAUD, AND HONOR

Some hymns are birthed out of wonderful ministries, such as those of Charles Wesley. Others result from times of great testing and hardship. The hymn, "All Glory, Laud, and Honor", was certainly produced during a time of great hardship and persecution. Written by Bishop Theodulf of Orleans, who was a confidant of Emperor Charlemagne during the Holy Roman Empire, Theodulf's fortunes shifted when Charlemagne's son ascended the throne. For some unsubstantiated reason, Theodulf fell under suspicion of treason by the brooding King Louis, and he was tossed into prison, where he was to languish for a good while. It was during those lonely years that Theodulf came up with the words of this hymn, first written down in Latin. The words speak of Jesus' triumphal entry into Jerusalem and are frequently associated with Palm Sunday, just before Easter. During his years or service and prominence under Charlemagne, Theodulf became the emperor's theological advisor, promoted education, founded schools, built chapels, wrote on a number of topics, and even translated a version of the Vulgate Bible. But at the same time as he was suffering in prison, this trial also brought to him a greater preciousness of the promise of eternal life, and it was at this time that he composed the hymn.

55 - THERE IS A FOUNTAIN FILLED WITH BLOOD

Some people seem to have it made in life...then there are others who never manage to get to first base. Or put another way, some folks seem to be dealt a winning hand...others...well, they're in trouble as soon as they show up for the game. William Cowper was one such soul. Living in England two hundred years ago, he appeared to have been dealt a winning hand. His father was a respected church clergyman, his mother from a family of royalty. But that's about as far as his good hand carried him. William's entire life was one of a tortured and crushed individual. What is truly remarkable, though, is what an amazing blessing he has been to all of us who have followed after him, right up to the present day. I have always marveled at how God seems to allow his choicest servants to be crushed, pulverized, and run through the mill...not because he is vindictive or is out to get us...but because he can and does use these folks in far greater ways than they could possibly imagine. Cowper took to writing poetry and hymns (between bouts of deep depression and attempts at suicide), and came up with two hymns that are still favorites and a blessing to us all even today. His two most popular hymns are: "God moves in a mysterious way", and "There is a fountain". This second one is perhaps based on Zechariah 13:1, which in the NIV reads, "On that day a fountain will be opened to the house of David and the inhabitants of Jerusalem, to cleanse them from sin and impurity." William understood well enough that he was a scoundrel deserving of God's greatest punishment. But one day his eyes were finally opened to what Christ had done for him. Jesus had poured out his own blood as a sacrifice so that William's sins (and the sins of all of us when we accept God's gift for us) could all be covered and washed away. What a glorious revelation, one that set William bursting forth in song. It can frighten me to think of what God allows people to go through and to endure at times. But Cowper's life is a good reminder to us that even the most difficult trials, God can redeem for good...and can keep using those trials to bless many who follow. This hymn was so greatly appreciated by Charles Spurgeon that he wanted one verse engraved on his tombstone: "E're since by faith I saw the stream, thy flowing wounds supply, redeeming love has been my theme, and shall be till I die."

56 - ANGELS FROM THE REALMS OF GLORY

James Montgomery had a tough beginning in life by any measure in the late 1700s. His parents felt a burden for the lost and so left their pastorate in Scotland for the island of Barbados as missionaries. Leaving behind their son, James, at the age of six, in the care of a Moravian community in Ireland, they struck out on their own. Shortly afterward, James was sent to a Moravian seminary in England, but he did not succeed academically. He abandoned this calling to become an apprentice baker and later a shop assistant. James never saw his parents again, as they passed away from yellow fever in Barbados several years later and so never returned home. Somewhere along the line, James discovered an enjoyment in writing, especially poetry. As things got tough, in order to survive, he would sell his poems on the streets of London. His wandering eventually took him to Sheffield where he found a job in the office of a newspaper, the Sheffield Register, which was known as a radical publication. The opportunity to help run the business of the newspaper and to write for its pages was exactly what he enjoyed and suited his gifting. When James was only 23 years old, the owner of the newspaper, after having been jailed several times, was driven out of town for his open stand in favor of Ireland's freedom from Great Britain. James eventually bought the newspaper when the owner had to flee the country to avoid again being put in prison, and he renamed it "The Sheffield Iris", using it to speak out against social injustice and slavery. Montgomery himself was imprisoned twice in York Castle for sensitive political articles and his activity as a leader in the abolitionist movement; once was for printing a song celebrating the Fall of the Bastille, and once for printing an account of a political riot in Sheffield. Slavery was legal at the time and Montgomery was using his paper to try and turn the tide against it and to set the slaves free. Following both times in prison, when he was released he went right back to the paper and fighting the war for two things: freedom for the slaves and freedom from Great Britain for the Irish. Despite the loss of his parents at such an early age, James Montgomery remained devoted to Christ and to the Scriptures, and he championed the cause of foreign missions and of the British Bible Society. As the years passed, he became a respected leader in Sheffield, and his writings were eagerly read by its citizens. On Christmas Eve, 1816, James opened his Bible to Luke 2 and was impacted by verse 13. Reflecting on the story of the angels, he started writing. By the end of the day, his new Christmas poem was being read in the newspaper. It was later set to music and was first sung on Christmas Day, 1821. The hymn invites people to "come and worship Christ the newborn King".

57 - OH COME, OH COME, EMMANUEL

Wouldn't it be fascinating to step back in time more than a thousand years and to listen to monks sing and chant this hymn back and forth to each other! This oldest of Christmas hymns that we sing originated in the 8th or 9th century as monks would sing it in Latin on the buildup to Christmas. The antiphons, as the verses beginning with "O" as called, point us to the coming of the Messiah.

The antiphons begin as follows:

O Sapentia (Wisdom)O Adonai (Hebrew for God)O Radix Jesse (root of Jesse)O Clavis David (key of David)O Oriens (dayspring)O Rex genitium (King of the Gentiles)O Emmanuel

What is interesting is that the first letter of the each word following the "O" spells SARCORE. If read backwards, the letters form a two word acrostic, "Ero cras," meaning, "I will be present tomorrow." I don't know how anyone managed to come up with that, or whether that was even the intention of the originator of this hymn...but an interesting element nonetheless.

Tradition suggests that this song began as a Benedictine Gregorian chant that, beginning the week before Christmas, the monks would sing a verse at a time to prepare their hearts and minds

LEWIS CODINGTON

for Christmas.

58 - I SING THE MIGHTY POWER OF GOD

Unusual for that day and age, over 300 years ago, Isaac Watts, known throughout England as a great hymn writer, possessed a passion to train children to sing as well. Nearly all hymns in those days, and certainly during my childhood also, we geared toward adults. But Watts knew that it was important to provide training for children, to teach them how to praise God as well. Toward this end, he labored on a hymnbook for children, which was published in the early 1700s. It was titled, "The Divine Songs for Children", and it included the hymn, "I Sing the Mighty Power of God". I don't recall it being considered a children's song when we sang it in church services in my childhood, so apparently somewhere along the way it was hijacked by adults and began appearing in their hymnbooks. I do remember singing it as a child, but never with the idea that it had actually been written for children. In this hymn, Watts hoped that the children who sang it would gain an understanding of God's love, his care, his goodness, and his power.

59 - I LOVE TO TELL THE STORY

Arabella Katherine Hankey was born in Clapham, near London, in 1834. She and her family were part of the Clapham group of evangelicals in England. They worked toward the abolition of slavery and the slave trade in support of William Wilberforce. They were also proponents of missionary work. At age 18, Kate moved closer into London to teach a Bible class for young ladies working in factories, and continued that work for more than a decade. Then at age 30, she became seriously ill. She was forced to rest in bed for a year. During that time of forced solitude, she wrote a long poem of 100 verses. Sometime later, the speaker at a convention happened to quote parts of her poem. Musician William Doane was in the audience at the time and was captivated by the poetry. After hearing Kate's poem, Doane turned part of it into the hymn, "Tell Me the Old, Old Story". Later, William Fischer did something similar with another part of Kate's poem. The result was the hymn, "I Love to Tell the Story". After recovering from her illness, Kate resumed her teaching ministry with factory girls and later began a prison ministry. Her life bore testimony to the fact that she loved both to hear and to tell the old, old story of Jesus and his love. Kate had also traveled to Africa to help out her missionary brother before she became ill. She never married, but spent her adult years in serving her Lord.

60 - WE'VE A STORY TO TELL

Henry Ernest Nichol was born in Yorkshire, England in 1862 and lived into his 60s. Perhaps the tumult of World War I, which he lived through, caused him to write this song of hope for the world – hope for peace based on a relationship with Jesus Christ. Nichol wrote 130 hymn tunes as well as many lyrics. In some instances, he used the pen name Colin Sterne – a rearrangement of the letters of his name, Ernest Nichol. This particular song was first published in 1896 in "Sunday School Hymnary" and is considered his most memorable. It encourages us to go out and teach all nations, as "We've A Story To Tell To The Nations". Originally intending to become an engineer, he abandoned this desire in order to study music. After receiving his degree from Oxford University in 1888, he produced a large number of melodies, the majority of which were for children's Sunday school services.

61 - NOW THANK WE ALL OUR GOD

The stories behind so many familiar hymns are fascinating...and are in many cases not at all familiar to us. I have heard and sung this hymn (Now thank we all our God) scores of times in the past, but don't recall ever hearing the amazing story behind it. Written nearly 400 years ago, it overflows with thankfulness to God for all of his goodness and bounty. One can only imagine that it was written in a wonderful time, during the best of circumstances...surely nothing like the grim situation facing many of us today. So was it written in such a time? Hardly. In the crucible of the European Thirty Years War, when enemies and attacks were surrounding the Germans on every side...and plagues, famine, and death were decimating them from within, it was actually composed during the worst of times imaginable. The writer, a Lutheran pastor named Martin Rinkart, resided in a little village by the name of Eilenberg, in Saxony, Germany, not too many miles from Czech and Poland, in the eastern portion of the country. In the early years of the 1600s, war erupted in that part of Europe as the forces of Sweden, France, Germany, and others collided, both over religious differences as well as for territorial greed. Upwards of five million or more people perished, most by disease, and in some areas nearly half the German inhabitants lost their lives. Rinkart, who grew up in poverty, felt called to the ministry and was just launching his pastoral career when conflict broke out all around him. The little town of Eilenberg, where he lived and served, was surrounded by a protective wall, and consequently, swarms of refugees flooded in as they attempted to escape the carnage. The Swedish army surrounded them, and in the crowded confines of the town, illness, starvation, and death increasingly began to visit them. One by one, local pastors perished along with the populace, until only Martin was left, toiling unceasingly to care for the suffering, some days conducting 50 funerals for the dead, including that of his own wife. Rinkart eventually helped to negotiate peace with the Swedes, and following the awful ordeal, he penned this hymn, which, next to Luther's "A Mighty Fortress", became the most frequently sung hymn in Germany. An amazing example to us still today, of giving thanks to God even in the midst of the worst suffering.

62 - ALL PEOPLE THAT ON EARTH DO DWELL

One of the oldest hymns still in use, this song first appeared in the Anglo-Genevan Psalter of 1561 and is attributed to the Scottish clergyman and Bible translator William Kethe. Earlier, Kethe fled to Switzerland from the persecution of Catholic Queen Mary in England. He helped with the translation of the Geneva Bible in 1560 and contributed 25 hymns to the Psalter, which he carried with him back to England in 1561, after the restoration of Protestantism there by Queen Elizabeth I. The text is based on the words of Psalm 100. Perhaps more famous and familiar than the hymn itself is the tune it is usually associated with, known as the "Old Hundredth", and which is also connected to Psalm 100. The hymn tune first appeared in the 1551 edition of the Genevan Psalter. The tunes in that Psalter became the source for the hymns of the Reformed churches in England and the Pilgrims in America. "All People That on Earth Do Dwell" was sung at the coronation of Queen Elizabeth II in 1953. As the Reformation spread, a revolution in songwriting occurred, and Christian musicians increasingly began to bless people by writing songs in their language. In England in the 1500s, the dominant strain of the Reformation was that of Calvin, who strongly advocated the singing of Psalms.

63 - NEARER, MY GOD, TO THEE

"Nearer My God to Thee" was written by British actress, poet, and hymn writer Sarah Flower Adams, who lived in the early 1800s. Her sister Eliza wrote the original music. After Adams' performance in London's 1837 play, "MacBeth", she received excellent reviews. Her desire was to continue with the theater into the future, but frail health put an end to her plans. And so she took to writing poems and hymns. Sarah's pastor was visiting the Adams family one afternoon and mentioned that he was having difficulty finding a hymn that represented his next week's sermon, taken from Genesis 28, and which recounts Jacob's dream. Sarah spontaneously volunteered to write a hymn for the service. Within a week, "Nearer My God to Thee" was composed. The beautiful hymn has spoken to many lives, and has even found its way into the theater that Adams so dearly loved. The song has been sung in several Hollywood films, including the Academy Award-winning films, "San Francisco", and "Titanic". One Canadian survivor of the 1912 Titanic tragedy recalled that the band played "Nearer My God to Thee" as the ship was sinking. In addition to this hymn, the sisters wrote 13 texts and 62 tunes for a hymnal published in 1841. The song did not gain great popularity until it was later joined with the present tune, composed especially for the text by Lowell Mason, who is sometimes known as the father of American church music. Sarah's sister Eliza, who was suffering from tuberculosis, died in 1846. Sarah had faithfully cared for her sister during the illness, but by the time Eliza died, Sarah, too, was showing signs of the disease. She herself passed away in 1848, at age 43. This hymn is associated with two US presidents. It was played as President James Garfield's body was laid to rest in 1881. And President William McKinley said that this was his favorite hymn. The hymn was sung at his funeral and at memorial services held across our land in 1901. "Nearer, My God, to Thee" has been used to bring spiritual comfort and blessing to many as it expresses the common yearning of people to know God and to experience His nearness and victory.

64 - ABIDE WITH ME

At age nine, Henry Lyte lost his parents and became an orphan. Robert Borrows, an Irish minister, took Henry in and raised him as his own child. He sent Lyte to school, and later Lyte followed his adoptive father's footsteps. After finishing his studies in 1814, he became a minister of a small village in Devonshire, England. Along its coast, Henry walked the trails and wrote most of his sermons, hymns, and poetry while out on these walks.

The death of one of his friends brought about a profound change in him when he went to his friend's bedside to offer him comfort. Neither he nor his dying friend had much within themselves that would give them peace in this situation. Through prayerful search of the Scriptures, they both came to a deeper faith in Christ, as Henry explained: "I was greatly affected by the whole matter, and brought to look at life and its issues with a different eye than before; and I began to study my Bible and preach in another manner than I had previously done." As a pastor, Lyte spent much of his time together with his wife caring for the sick. Eventually he developed tuberculosis, which was close to a death sentence at the time. As his health weakened, Lyte delivered his farewell sermon to his congregation in 1847. Along with it, he shared the lyrics to the hymn, "Abide with Me", which he had written. Several weeks after preaching his last sermon, Lyte died at age of 54. Since that time, the song has appeared in nearly every hymn book in the English language.

65 - COME, YE THANKFUL PEOPLE, COME

Anyone in a farming environment knows the importance of a good harvest.

This really calls for thanksgiving to the great Provider as reflected in the hymn, "Come, ye thankful people, come". Although we think of this hymn as being particularly for the Thanksgiving season, it's message is actually broader than thanking God for the blessing of a good harvest. It was written by Henry Alford during his pastorate of a small country church in England. While using words that speak of the harvest, it also refers to the parables of the wheat and the tares (Matthew 13:24-30) and the sower (Mark 4:26-29). Alford was a scholar poet who wrote and published hymns relating to the Christian year. When Henry was only 16 years old, he wrote this statement: "I do this day, in the presence of God and my own soul, renew my covenant with God and solemnly determine henceforth to become His, and to do His work as far as in me lies." Alford was born in London in 1810. He was nurtured by Christian parents and though he lost his mother at a young age, he was greatly influenced by a father and grandfather who were Anglican pastors. Their example guided him into a personal commitment to Jesus Christ. His religious development was such that he wrote an outstanding, short sermon at age 10. After he graduated from Trinity College and was ordained in 1833, he combined his ministry work with teaching, and he founded a choral group for the development of music and the performance of oratorios in Canterbury Cathedral. Henry Alford played the piano and organ and could sing very well. He also published a few Latin odes and a history of the Jews. One of his greatest works was the Greek Testament in four volumes, which was first published in 1849 and is still available today. He married his cousin Fanny Alford in 1836. Together they had four children. However, he lost both of his sons at a young age. His two daughters survived and were married during his lifetime. Alford was eventually appointed Dean of Canterbury Cathedral, known as the mother church of England. He produced one of the most memorable songs of thanksgiving in the beautiful words that he composed in this hymn. It reflects on the harvest when the Lord will come again and gather all his children home. In 1870, Henry Alford suffered a physical breakdown due to his strenuous activities in the ministry. He died the next year. His death at age 61 left a void in the hearts of many people whom God had touched through his ministry. The Christian harvest festival in England is a special occasion of thanksgiving to the Lord for the abundant harvest. For this particular occasion, Alford was inspired to write the text of this hymn. It first appeared in his book, "Psalms and Hymns".

66 - SILENT NIGHT

This most popular of Christmas hymns was first produced in a time of trauma and suffering in Europe, over 200 years ago. It was intended to turn the people's focus to what is most important, the peace and salvation brought to us by Jesus. During our present day of suffering, confusion, and uncertainty, we, too, are needing the message and reminder that this hymn brings to us. The story of "Stille Nacht" is one of the most well known among the traditional hymns, though it is sometimes hard to sort out truth from fantasy with regard to the hymn's origin. Joseph Mohr was an Austrian cathedral choir member in Salzburg, Austria, as a boy. He was born into a very poor family and eventually adopted as a foster child by the local Catholic cathedral. He was trained to become a priest and developed a deep love of music. He later became an assistant priest at the St. Nicholas Church in Oberndorf, Austria. Mohr was ordained as a Catholic priest in 1815. He spent most of his life ministering in parishes near Salzburg. Living a simple life, he died in poverty after giving away what little he had to the poor. In 1816, Mohr wrote the original six stanzas of the poem that would make him famous around the world. Franz Gruber was an Austrian worship leader and school teacher, holding church positions near Salzburg. While a successful composer, little was published and none of his works are known today except for this Christmas carol. Tradition has it that the carol was composed for a text by his assistant priest Joseph Mohr on short notice for the Christmas Eve Mass in Oberndorf in 1818. Though a guitar was not the normal instrument for services, it was used in this case to great effect. Against the general mood of oppression at the time, Mohr and Gruber wanted to give some hope. Mohr wrote the song's lyrics in the form of a poem amid this dark time, literally, for Austria. The volcanic eruption of Mount Tambora, one of the most powerful in recorded history, darkened the skies with ash, lowered temperatures, killed crops and caused famine throughout 1816, which became known as "The Year Without a Summer". Austrians also felt battered and exhausted from years of conflict that claimed many lives, damaged the economy, killed jobs, and left the landscape littered with crumbled buildings and homes. Father Mohr faced a congregation of traumatized people, and his text for 'Silent Night' was likely intended to offer peace and comfort during great hardship. On December 24, 1818, Mohr gave Gruber a copy of his poem, "Silent Night". He asked him to put it to music for the Christmas celebration that evening, as a last minute music change was needed because of a malfunctioning organ! Later that day, the now famous notes were complete. Christmas Eve celebrates the coming birth of Jesus, but on that occasion it was also the first time "Silent Night" in German was ever performed.

67 - O LITTLE TOWN OF BETHLEHEM

I remember the impact it had on us when my wife and I visited Bethlehem a few years back…to think that Jesus had actually been born right there…and how it changed the whole course of history, and not just on Christmas. It had a profound impact on Philip Brooks when he also visited Bethlehem (on horseback, no less!) more than 150 years ago. I can't say that my visit led me to write a hymn about the experience, but in Brooks' case it did; in fact, it became one of the best loved hymns that we still today associate with the Christmas season. Born in Boston in 1835, Brooks was one of six sons, four of whom entered the ministry. Following studies at Harvard and beyond, he accepted a position in the Boston Latin School, an institution he himself had attended. However, unable to manage a class of unruly teenagers, he resigned after only six months. Frustrated by that experience, Brooks began preparing instead for the ministry. His first assignment was in Philadelphia. He was an immediate success as a preacher and attracted large crowds. Three years later, in 1862, he was invited to be the minister of Holy Trinity Church in his hometown of Boston. When President Lincoln was assassinated in 1865,

Brooks was invited to deliver a eulogy at his Philadelphia funeral service. That same year, having become exhausted and depleted from his ministry, he took a sabbatical and, while touring the Middle East, visited Jerusalem. On Christmas Eve he borrowed a horse and made the six mile journey to Bethlehem to worship in the Church of the Nativity. Later, he wrote in his journal: "I was standing in the old church in Bethlehem, close to the spot where Jesus was born, when the whole church was ringing hour after hour with the splendid hymns of praise...telling each other of the Savior's birth." When he returned home, he told friends that the Christmas Eve experience would forever be "singing in my soul". Three years later, as the Christmas season again came around, Brooks thought back to his very moving experience in Bethlehem. As those memories came back to him again, he began writing a poem for the church Christmas program. He hurried to show the poem to his friend, Lewis Redner, the organist at Holy Trinity Church. Redner was asked to compose a simple tune to accompany his words that children could sing. Though at first struggling to put together a suitable melody, one night Redner was awakened from his sleep with a tune in his head. He later told friends that the music was a gift from God. The carol became a favorite of children and adults alike. It was an immediate hit. Other churches began using it, delighting worshippers who were enamored with the words and the tune. During the following several years, "O Little Town of Bethlehem" was the most popular Christmas carol in Philadelphia, and was used in almost every church during their Christmas services. Though Phillips Brooks wrote several other Christmas and Easter hymns, only "O Little Town of Bethlehem" survived the test of time and continues to be sung in churches all over the world. As well as being an effective communicator from the pulpit, Brooks also published a number of books on preaching and the life of Christ. In 1880 he became the first American invited to preach for the Queen of England.

68 - BE STILL, MY SOUL

In Mark 4, Jesus shows his power over nature, while he and his disciples encountered a storm on the Sea of Galilee. "Teacher, do You not care that we are perishing?", cried his men. In response, we are told, "He arose and rebuked the wind, and said to the sea, 'Peace, be still!' And the wind ceased and there was a great calm." Similar thoughts led to the creation of a truly great hymn. Katharina von Schlegel wrote 29 hymns. "Be Still, My Soul" was produced in 1752. The strength of faith and depth of feeling it expresses make it one of our most beloved hymns.

Following centuries of stagnation in the church during the Middle Ages, congregational singing experienced a rebirth toward the end of the 17th century, when spiritual revival started with a force known as the Pietistic movement in the Lutheran church in Germany. This occurrence was similar to the Puritan and Wesleyan movements in England. A pastor of a church in Berlin, Philipp Spener, was the leader of this German renewal. He was not a hymn writer himself but greatly encouraged singing which led to a revival in singing hymns in Germany during that time. The hymns from this movement were characterized with rich

Christian experience, piety, and faithfulness in the Scriptures. The hymn writer, Katharina von Schlegel (born in 1697), was an outstanding figure during this spiritual revival. Little is known of her other than that she was a Lutheran, and likely of aristocratic birth. She died about 1768. Katharina's life was characterized by a focus on the study of God's Word, as well living it out in daily life. Katharina's hymn, "Be Still, My Soul", is a prayer to patiently put our trust in the Lord even in times of trouble. It shows us that no matter what we may go through, ultimately there is a joyful end to our sufferings. That ought to give us a blessed assurance that, no matter what, God is on our side. He always has been and always will be.

69 – I SURRENDER ALL

Judson Van DeVenter was born in 1855 and grew up on a farm in Michigan. After attending Hillsdale College, he became an art teacher. At the same time, Judson began volunteering at his church, and it was soon apparent that God had gifted him for evangelism. Though he was encouraged to pursue full-time ministry, Judson struggled with the idea of giving up his career in art. Eventually, he did "surrender all" and later shared an account of the writing of this well known hymn: "The song was written while I was conducting a meeting at East Palestine, Ohio. For some time, I had struggled between developing my talents in the field of art and going into full-time evangelistic work. At last the pivotal hour of my life came, and I surrendered all. A new day was ushered into my life. I became an evangelist and discovered down deep in my soul a talent hitherto unknown to me. God had hidden a song in my heart, and touching a tender chord, he caused me to sing." Around 1896, Judson began to travel across the US, England, and Scotland as an evangelist, along with Winfield Weeden, who wrote the music for "I Surrender All". In his retirement, Judson began a radio program called "The Gospel in Song and Story", and around 1923, he became a professor of hymnology at the Florida

Bible Institute. A student at the college would later recall the meaningful time that he had at Judson's home in fellowship and singing. This student also mentioned the significant influence that Judson had on his life – so much so that he also became an evangelist; his name was Billy Graham! Graham related, "We students loved this kind, deeply spiritual gentleman and often gathered in his home for an evening of fellowship and singing."

Billy Graham was with the hymn writer when he died on July 17, 1939. "He went to be with Christ with a smile on his face, looking forward to seeing Jesus," Graham said, recounting that Van DeVenter sang "I Surrender All" on his deathbed.

70 - HOW GREAT THOU ART

In 1885, Carl Boberg was walking home in Sweden, returning from a service with his friends in the seaside town of Mönsterås. Boberg shared this story from that day: "A thunderstorm began to appear on the horizon. We hurried to shelter. There were loud claps of thunder, and the lightning flashed across the sky. Strong winds swept over the meadows and billowing fields of grain. However, the storm was soon over and the clear sky appeared with a beautiful rainbow." After he reached his home, he opened "the window toward the sea. The church bells were playing the tune of a hymn". That same evening he sat down and wrote "O Store Gud" - the poem that would eventually become "How Great Thou Art". The hymn was not well known until it was translated into German in 1907 and then brought to Russia in 1912. Stuart K. Hine, an English missionary, learned it in Russian and translated it, adding the fourth stanza in 1948. Over the years this beautiful hymn has been translated into many languages reaching the people of God, uniting them in a single voice to praise the Almighty Creator. The last verse was inspired by displaced Russians who had experienced great suffering but looked forward to seeing their loved ones again in heaven.

71 - MY JESUS, I LOVE THEE

"My Jesus I Love Thee" is a wonderful expression of love for Jesus that comes out of the author's experience of the Savior's love for him. It was written as a devotional poem by Willam Ralph Featherston, a teenager who had recently given his life to Jesus. Not much is known about Featherston, except that he attended a Methodist church in Montreal, that he was young when he wrote the poem (12 or 16 years old), and that he died at just 27 years of age. One story about how the poem became public is that Featherston mailed it to his aunt in Los Angeles who then looked for a way to have it published. It wasn't until after Featherston's death that Adoniram Judson Gordon (founder of Gordon College and Gordon-Conwell Theological Seminary) added a melody and published it in his book of hymns. As we sing Featherson's words we are all able to declare our relationship with Christ, to sing of our assurance of salvation, to celebrate the Gospel, to express joy in Christ's love, and to seek to praise Christ in all circumstances. Eventually, it ended up in a book called "The London Hymn Book" as an anonymous hymn in 1864, giving it a wider audience among the public. One story is told of an actress who stopped in to see a sick girl, hoping her presence would cheer the child. But the girl was a devout Christian, and suggested that the actress give serious thought to becoming a Christian. The actress soon became a follower of Christ. She had to tell her father, who was also her manager, that she had to abandon acting, since she could not be an actress and a follower of Christ. Her father was horrified, and explained that her decision would bring the ruin of their whole business. The actress decided to relent and preparations for her next big performance continued. She was the star of a theater production. The evening came and the father was so happy his daughter had not destroyed their income. When the curtain was raised, the actress stepped forward to the applause and music of a huge crowd. But instead of starting with her lines, she began to sing, "My Jesus, I Love Thee". Her father later did get saved and many others came to salvation through her testimony.

72 - ALL FOR JESUS

Mary D. James began teaching Sunday School at the age of 13 in her local Methodist Episcopal Church in New Jersey. She became a well known figure in the Wesleyan Holiness movement of the early 1800s, leading meetings and submitting articles to several Christian publications. Along with having a family with four children, Mary strived to live a life as close to Christ as possible. She wrote "All For Jesus" as a New Year's resolution in 1871. As she wrote the letter, she expressed thankfulness in the work for her Lord that she was involved in during the previous year. She wrote, "I have written more, talked more, prayed more, and thought more for Jesus than in any previous year, and have had more peace of mind, resulting from a stronger and more simple faith in Him." She saw how her increased commitment to God gave her a stronger ministry. May we all experience the same realization! "All For Jesus" was a personal expression of her devotion to God, conveying her desire that all she was going to do in the years to come would be for His glory.

73 - FOR THE BEAUTY OF THE EARTH

Folliott Pierpoint was born in England in 1835. After graduating from Cambridge, he taught at Somersetshire College. He wrote hymns for several publications and published two songbooks. He wrote numerous poems, but "For the Beauty of the Earth" is the one we still remember him for today. The hymn was written to celebrate the Lord's Supper. Pierpoint wrote the song as he was inspired by the beauty of the countryside around Bath, in the southwest of England. In addition to the beautiful countryside with its winding, peaceful Avon River, the songbirds and the wind flowing over the colorful hillside all seemed to be praising the Creator with their overflowing joy and peace. Staggered by all he saw around him, Pierpoint expressed his feelings of gratitude in the sentiments of this song. He mentions many aspects of the world for which he is grateful, including the earth and skies, trees and flowers, human love, and our gracious Heavenly Father. This joyful hymn is a wonderful reminder of all the beauty God has poured into his world around us.

74 - BLESSED ASSURANCE

"Blessed Assurance" was written by Fanny Crosby in 1873. Fanny Crosby was a prolific hymn writer who also happened to be blind. Frances Jane Crosby was born in New York state on March 24, 1820. She became blind at the age of six weeks from mistreatment of her eyes during a sickness. At the age of 15, she entered the New York Institution for the Blind, where she became a teacher in 1847. She taught English grammar, rhetoric, and American history. While there, she met Presidents Van Buren and Tyler, as well as other famous Americans. Concerning Henry Clay, she commented: "When Mr. Clay came to the institution during his last visit to New York, I was selected to welcome him with a poem. Six months before he had lost a son at the battle of Monterey, and I had sent him some verses. In my address I carefully avoided any allusion to them, in order not to wound him. When I had finished he drew my arm in his, and, addressing the audience, said through his tears: 'This is not the first poem for which I am indebted to this lady. Six months ago she sent me some lines on the death of my dear son.' Both of us were overcome for a few moments. Soon, by a splendid effort, Mr. Clay recovered

himself, but I could not control my tears." Fanny Crosby also had the honor of being the first woman to speak to the Senate in Washington, reading one of her poems before the assembly. In addition to the thousands of hymns that she wrote (about 8,000 poems in all), she published four volumes of verses. Though these show the poetical bent of her mind, they have little to do with her world-wide fame. It is as a writer of songs and Gospel hymns that she is known. Fanny was married on March 5, 1858, to Alex Van Alstyne, who was also a blind instructor in the same institution in which she taught. She began to write Sunday school hymns for William Bradbury in 1864. Her first hymn, "We are going, we are going to a home beyond the skies", was sung at Mr. Bradbury's funeral in 1868. After 1864 she supported herself by writing hymns. She could compose at any time and did not need to wait for any special inspiration, with many of her best hymns coming on the spur of the moment. "Safe in the arms of Jesus", probably one of her best known hymns, was her own favorite. Fanny loved her work, and was happy in it. The secret of this contentment dates from her first composition at the age of eight. "It has been the motto of my life," she said. It is:
"O what a happy soul am I!
Although I cannot see,
I am resolved that in this world
Contented I will be."
This continued to be her philosophy. She believed

that if she had not been blind, she might not have received such a good education or had such a good memory. She knew much of the Bible by heart, and had committed to memory the first four books of the Old Testament and the four Gospels before she was ten years old. Although most of Fanny's hymns appeared under the name of Fanny J. Crosby or Mrs. Yan Alstyne, she also used nearly 200 different names, partly to deflect attention from herself. She produced as many as seven hymn-poems in one day. On several occasions, after hearing an unfamiliar hymn sung, she would ask about the author, and discover that it was one of her own! Fanny never felt any resentment against the doctor who mistreated her eyes, but believed it was permitted by the Lord to fulfill His plan for her life. Her wise mother prepared her daughter for a contented life, in spite of this great handicap. And her grandmother became an unforgettable influence in her life. Her grandmother spent many hours describing nature and heaven to Fanny. Her grandmother told her that she would most likely not receive an education like other children, so she would need to remember as much as she could of everything she heard. Also, she introduced Fanny to the Bible and it became more familiar to her than any other source of information. It provided the themes, inspiration, and diction for her gospel hymns. Fanny could not write, although she did learn how to sign her name. She could not read Braille because the tips of her fingers were so calloused from playing the guitar and harp. There was one occasion when Fanny had over 40 hymns in her memory before she could get to someone who could write them down for her. For her living expenses, she was under a contract to write three hymns per week at the rate of $2 per hymn. In order to accomplish this, the publishers hired a secretary to live with Fanny and write down all of the hymns that came to her mind. The epitaph on Fanny Crosby's tombstone reads, "Aunt Fanny — Blessed assurance, Jesus is mine. Oh, what a foretaste of glory divine."

On one occasion, Fanny's friend Phoebe Knapp, played a tune for Fanny and asked her what the tune said to her. Fanny listened and replied, "It says, "Blessed assurance, Jesus is mine." The rest of the words for this hymn just flowed from her. Fanny Crosby was upbeat about her blindness, once saying, "I believe that God intended that I should live my days in physical darkness so that I might be better prepared to sing his praise and lead others from spiritual darkness into eternal light. With sight I would have been too distracted to have written thousands of hymns."

75 - I STAND AMAZED AT THE PRESENCE

In the early 1900s, Charles H. Gabriel (1856-1932) was the king of Gospel music. He wrote the words and music for many of the hymns used by popular evangelists of his day, such as Billy Sunday. Charles' hymns reflected a change in the style of Gospel music. In the 1800s, hymns were more theological and meditative. But with the revivals of Moody and Sunday, Christians learned to love songs that were fun to sing, highly energetic, and easy to remember. Charles is credited with between 7,000-8,000 songs. And he wrote tunes for other songs as well, including "His Eye Is On the Sparrow" and "Will the Circle Be Unbroken?" But the hymn that seems to have had the longest life is the hymn, "I Stand Amazed in the Presence", which sounds like it could have been written today. This hymn focuses on a single thought...amazement and gratitude at the incredible sacrifice of Christ for our atonement. Charles Gabriel was born in Iowa and raised on a farm. He taught himself to play his family's reed organ and never had any formal music training. Gabriel focused his attention on the One who had gifted him musically, not on himself as a condemned sinner. Gabriel evidently had emerged from his own struggles – including his father's death when he was still a teenager, and his failed first marriage - to recognize the Lord's work in his life. His mother challenged him to make a habit of scribbling down his own words and music after finishing his farm work each day. In response to the boy's wish to become famous, she said, "I would rather have you write a song that will help somebody than see you become President of the United States." Her hopes for her son came true, and Charles Gabriel became known as the "Master of Missionary Music". Gabriel led worship for Billy Sunday and encouraged listeners to hear the "Macedonian call" and to send the Light around the world. One common thread throughout many of Gabriel's lyrics is the high honor and sense of indebtedness to spread the Gospel.

76 - TO GOD BE THE GLORY

A hymn which expresses glory to the Lord and which encourages us to give him honor is, "To God Be The Glory". The text was written by Fanny Crosby (1820-1915). It was first published in the 1875 collection, "Brightest and Best". Also included in that collection were "All the Way My Savior Leads Me", "I Am Thine, O Lord", "Savior, More Than Life to Me", and "Christ Arose". However, "To God Be the Glory" was almost totally unknown in America until fairly recently. Ira Sankey sang it in the Dwight L. Moody evangelistic campaigns, and he included it in his "Sacred Songs and Solos", which was published in England and is still in use today. But after that, it faded from public use until Cliff Barrows was given a copy in 1954 and began to popularize it during the Billy Graham crusades in London. Barrows was impressed with its strong message of praise and included it in the songbook being prepared for the services and used it in the crusade. The crowds responded so enthusiastically that he sang it nearly every night. Later, Graham and Barrows introduced the song in the U.S. for the first time at their Nashville Crusade. The crowd again responded well, so the song was adopted as one of the standards for future campaigns. Because of the influence of Billy Graham, the compilers of hymnals began including it in new publications, and thus it became widely popular. Students of Fanny Crosby's hymns point out that this song differs from many of her other hymns because it is not so much a personal testimony as many of her others are, but rather contains more of a theological message to it. Carl Daw noted that "this is a remarkably objective celebration of God's saving work in Jesus Christ".

77 - IN THE CROSS OF CHRIST

An accomplished linguist, John Bowring was perhaps fluent in over 20 languages and able to speak 80 more. He was also one of the preeminent British statesmen of his day, serving in numerous positions across the globe: Commissioner to France, Consul at Canton, Minister Plenipotentiary to China, Governor of Hong Kong, and twice a member of Parliament. Queen Victoria knighted him in 1854. Yet in spite of all his service, and the fact that he had 36 published volumes, he is best known for this single hymn text. On his tombstone are the words from his famous hymn: "In the Cross of Christ I Glory." In the apostle Paul's day, the Greeks viewed the story of a Savior dying on a cross as a foolish notion. But in the early 19th century, John Bowring clearly had a different attitude when he wrote the hymn, "In the Cross of Christ I Glory". The fact that it sounds strange to modern ears demonstrates the change in the spiritual landscape of our world in the last 200 years. The title and first line are based on the words of Paul in Galatians 6:14: "But God forbid that I should glory, save in the cross of our Lord Jesus Christ, by whom the world is crucified unto me, and I unto the world." So why would Paul glory/rejoice/boast in the cross of Christ, with the cross being the most lowly and disgraceful death of that time? After all, most of the world saw only curses in the cross. All Scripture centers around the cross of Christ when we recognize that the slain lamb of the sacrifices exemplified the death of Christ on the cross. Christ was the "Lamb slain from the foundation of the world", and John the Baptist recognized him as the fulfillment of the whole sacrificial system when he exclaimed, "Behold the Lamb of God which takes away the sin of the world!" The eternal Son knew even before he came to earth the scorn and suffering he would meet, but he also knew that many would receive him as Savior. And that is why he came to earth to die on our behalf and thus reveal the love of God for humanity.

78 - I AM THINE, O LORD

The man who composed the music to this hymn had many interests in addition to Gospel music. He was an inventor, a businessman who owned a large machine factory, and a civic leader. But what William Doane enjoyed the most was serving in the Sunday School program in his church...and writing music. He became Fanny Crosby's main partner in writing Gospel songs, and they were personal friends as well. One evening, as Fanny Crosby visited William in his home in Cincinnati, they were talking about the wonderful privilege of being able to experience and enjoy being near to God, to feel His presence, and to delight in His love. Suddenly, Fanny, the famous blind songwriter, stopped talking and said she had an idea for a song. Word for word, she dictated the song to William. The next morning, he came up with a tune to go with the song. Those words and that tune became the well loved hymn, "I am thine, O Lord". Crosby likely drew her inspiration from several Bible passages:

Hebrews 10:22

"Let us draw near with a true heart in full assurance of faith, having our hearts sprinkled from an evil conscience, and our bodies washed

with pure water."
Hebrews 10:19
"Having therefore, brethren, boldness to enter into the holiest by the blood of Jesus."
James 4:8
"Draw nigh to God, and he will draw nigh to you. Cleanse your hands, ye sinners; and purify your hearts, ye double minded."
As is typical of Crosby's hymns, she wrote in the first person, making this a very personal statement of faith. This is reflective of the revivalist tradition at the time. Her hymns strongly expressed the personal aspect of her relationship with her Savior and her heart felt response to that commitment.

79 – I COME TO THE GARDEN ALONE

Austin Miles shared his memory of how the words to this hymn came to him, in the account which follows: "One day in April 1912, I was seated in the dark room where I kept my photographic equipment, and also my organ. I drew my Bible toward me, and it opened at my favorite book and chapter, John chapter twenty. I don't know if this was by chance or by the work of the Holy Spirit. That story of Jesus and Mary had lost none of its power and charm. It was as though I was in a trance; as I read it that day, I seemed to be part of the scene. I became a silent witness to that dramatic moment in Mary's life when she knelt before her Lord and cried, 'Rabboni'. I rested my hands on the open Bible, as I stared at the light blue wall. As the light faded, I seemed to be standing at the entrance of a garden, looking down a gently winding path, shaded by olive branches. A woman in white, with head bowed, hand clasping her throat as if to choke back her sobs, walked slowly into the shadows. It was Mary. As she came to the tomb, upon which she placed her hand, she bent over to look in and ran away. Then came Peter, who entered the tomb, followed by John. As they departed, Mary reappeared leaning her head on her arm at the tomb, and she wept. Turning, she saw Jesus standing there; so did I. I knew it was he. She knelt before him, with arms outstretched, and looking into his face cried, 'Rabboni'. I awakened in sunlight, gripping my Bible and wrote, as quickly as the words could be formed, the lyrics exactly as it is sung today. That same evening, I wrote the tune. It is sung today as it was written in 1912." Miles hoped to capture in his words the closeness Mary might have felt to her Savior at that moment. He thought, "This is not an experience limited to a happening almost 2000 years ago, but it is the daily companionship with the Savior that makes up the Christian's daily walk."

A Chinese pastor also shared his experience in relation to this same hymn. He had been incarcerated in a detention camp during the Cultural Revolution. Each day he was lowered into a pit filled with human waste and ordered to start shoveling. He was able to endure this horrific indignity by singing over and over again the words to "I Come to the Garden Alone". He refused to allow his captors to define his reality; rather, he chose to see himself as enjoying the presence of his Savior. C. Austin Miles lived from 1868 to 1946. He trained and worked as a pharmacist, but also began to write Gospel songs when he was 24 years old. His song was published by the Hall-Mack company, and then Miles gave up his pharmacy work to serve Hall-Mack as an editor and manager for nearly 40 years. He said once, "It is as a writer of Gospel songs I am proud to be known, for in that way I may be of the most use of my Master, whom I serve willingly although not as efficiently as I desire."

80 - MORE ABOUT JESUS

Eliza Hewitt wrote "More About Jesus" in 1887. She was born in 1851 in Philadelphia, Pennsylvania, and was trained in education, later becoming a schoolteacher in the public schools in Philadelphia. One day, Eliza was struck in the back with a heavy slate by one of her students who was very distraught. Seriously injured, Eliza was unable to go back to teaching; but she did continue to be involved in Sunday School. She spent most of the time following her injury indoors. While slowly recovering, she studied literature and wrote poems for her church. At one point, she had a class with as many as 200 children. She was able in that situation to combine the two great loves of her life: children and Jesus. She later became superintendent of the primary department of the church when her condition improved. Even though she was able to work to some degree, Eliza still was in constant pain for the rest of her life. "More about Jesus" was one of the poems she wrote while she was incapacitated. It expresses her desire to know Jesus better, as is expressed in Philippians 3:10: "I want to know Christ and the power of His resurrection..." Through her pain, her attention was turned, and she desired to know more of Jesus. May this be the desire of all of us.

81 - HIS EYE IS ON THE SPARROW

This song was written by Civilla Martin in 1905. Civilla was married to William Martin, an evangelist. While in New York, in 1905, the couple became friends with the Doolittles. Mrs. Doolittle had been bedridden for 20 years and her husband was crippled and in a wheelchair. Civilla wrote: "Despite their afflictions, they lived happy Christian lives, bringing inspiration and comfort to all who knew them. One day, while we were visiting the Doolittles, my husband commented on their bright hopefulness and asked them for the secret of it. Mrs. Doolittle's reply was simple: 'His eye is on the sparrow, and I know he watches me.' The beauty of this simple expression of boundless faith gripped the hearts and fired the imagination of Dr. Martin and me. The song, 'His Eye is on the Sparrow', was the outcome of that experience."

82 - COME, THOU LONG EXPECTED JESUS

In 1744, hymn writer and preacher Charles Wesley thought about the situation of orphans in the area surrounding him, as well as the serious class divide in Britain at the time. As he reflected on the promise of a Savior who would bring deliverance, described in God's Word, these words came together in his mind: "Born your people to deliver, born a child and yet a King, born to reign in us forever, now your gracious kingdom bring. By your own eternal Spirit, rule in all our hearts alone; by your all sufficient merit, raise us to your glorious throne." Wesley adapted this prayer into a hymn and published it in his "Hymns for the Nativity of our Lord" songbook. The little collection was so popular that it was reprinted 20 times during Wesley's lifetime. The hymn spread throughout England and was made popular by Charles Spurgeon to a wider audience. Wesley did not want to just paint a picture of Jesus in the manger; he wanted the entire Christmas story to have a personal application. He wanted to impress upon God's people that Jesus is not only the "desire of every nation", but is also the personal "joy of every longing heart". Jesus has the "government on his shoulders", but he was born to reign personally "in us".

83 - I HEARD THE BELLS ON CHRISTMAS DAY

"I Heard the Bells on Christmas Day" is a carol based on the poem, "Christmas Bells", by Henry Wadsworth Longfellow.

The song tells of hearing Christmas bells during the American Civil War, but at the same time, despairing that "hate is strong and mocks the song of peace on earth, good will to men". After much anguish and despondency, the carol concludes with the statement that "God is not dead, nor doth He sleep", and that there will ultimately be "peace on earth, good will to men". On December 25, 1863, Longfellow, widowed twice and with six children, wrote a poem capturing the turmoil in his heart as well as in the world he observed around him at that moment. He heard church bells ringing in Cambridge and the singing of "peace on earth" (Luke 2:14), but what he saw was a world of injustice and violence that on the surface seemed to mock the truthfulness of this optimistic outlook.

Two years earlier, his wife had been burned to death in a fire, and he was also badly burned trying to save her, requiring him to cover his face with a beard from then on. At times, his grief was so great that he wondered whether he would be sent to an asylum. Previously, his first wife died following a miscarriage. Apart from Longfellow's hope in God's eternal promises, it might have been easy for him to give up all hope.

84 – IT CAME UPON A MIDNIGHT CLEAR

This Christmas hymn was written by Edmund Sears, a minister in Massachusetts, in 1849. The words focus on the angels who appeared in Bethlehem at the time of Jesus' birth and their message of peace...personal peace, spiritual peace, and also peace in society, as the rumblings of the US Civil War grew louder. It was a troubled time. The California Gold Rush was creating excitement, but was also disrupting the lives of men and women caught up in Gold Fever. The Industrial Revolution was pulling people away from their small farms to the cities, where they often just exchanged one form of poverty for another. And, of course, the tensions over slavery, which would soon plunge the nation into a terrible war, were already present. In that troubled context, Sears wrote this hymn that emphasizes peace as a gift from "heaven's all-gracious king". He portrays angels bringing peace to a still-weary world - angels hovering above "sad and lowly plains". Sears pictures a painful view of life, with its "crushing load"...and "painful steps"...and a "weary road"... but offers the hope of "glad and golden hours" that will "come swiftly on the wing". And he looks forward to the fulfillment of prophecy: "When the new heaven and earth shall own the Prince of Peace their King". This wonderful message of faith, given to us in Luke 2, tells the good news of the angels: "Glory to God in the highest, and on earth, peace, good will toward all men." Despite being written in 1849, the words are as relevant today as at that moment. Instead of focusing on Bethlehem and the details of the nativity scene, this poem draws our attention to the message of the angels. The first verse lays out the scene of the angels "bending near the earth" on that clear night, and each of the following verses pictures the angels whose heavenly music still "floats o'er all the weary world". This carol is not so much about the baby Jesus as it is about the anticipation of the promised peace of Christ and the difference this peace will make in the world, when we listen to the angels' song. As he struggled to write his Christmas Eve sermon that year, "it was the poverty and the hopelessness of the people he touched in the slums that sickened his heart and blocked his progress. He must have wondered how he could write about the Light of the world when the world seemed so very dark". There was something about who the angels announced the birth to that inspired Sears. The angels came to the lowly, the marginalized – the shepherds. And in his mind, they come and sing over us still today. As a minister deeply committed to social causes, he understood the importance of hope, the importance of purpose – the importance of trusting that things can and will get better.

85 - WHAT CHILD IS THIS

William Chatterton Dix (1837-1898) was born in Bristol, England. His father, a surgeon, had written a biography of the poet, Thomas Chatterton, which accounts for the middle name that he gave his son. It also reveals the affection for poetry that his father passed on to William. When he was young, William moved to Glasgow, Scotland, where he eventually was managing an insurance company. However, his real passion was poetry. When he was 29, Dix became seriously ill, and was bedridden for an extended period of time which caused him to slip into depression. Dix then called out to God and "met Him in a new and real way". Out of this spiritual experience, he began to write many poems and hymns, including this carol, and also read a good bit of Christian material. He came through the crisis with a deeper faith, and devoted much of his later poetry to Christian themes. At least three of the hymns he wrote at the time have survived to this day, the other two being, "As with Gladness, Men of Old" and "Alleluia! Sing to Jesus". "What Child Is This?" came from a longer poem, "The Manger Song". It was published in 1865 in Britain, and then became popular in the US as well. The melody is a traditional English folk tune. Dix continued to write, and over the course of his life, produced more than 40 hymns. Of all his work, the song, "What Child Is This?", has been the most lasting. Each stanza is a progression – the words start by asking about the divinity of baby Jesus and finish by praising his name.

86 - JESUS IS ALL THE WORLD TO ME

Will Thompson was a popular song writer, and at the age of sixteen wrote "Darling Minnie Gray" and "The Liverpool Schottische". Both songs were published, and he was on his way to a career in secular music. But he later committed his life to the service of Christ and focused on writing hymns. His best known creation is the song of invitation, "Softly and Tenderly Jesus Is Calling". Will Thompson (1847-1909) was born in Pennsylvania, and his family moved to Ohio while he was still young. His father was a businessman and served in the Ohio legislature. Thompson developed an early interest in music, and wrote several songs before finishing high school. Thompson first graduated from Alliance College and then later graduated from the New England Conservatory of Music as well as studying music in Leipzig, Germany. As a young man, Thompson sent a package of four songs to a publisher, asking payment of $100 for the package of four. The publisher responded with a counter-offer of $25, which Thompson declined. When he couldn't get what he considered to be a fair price for his music, Thompson decided to go into business for himself. He started a music store in East Liverpool in association with his father's business - and another outlet in Chicago. Then he went into the mail order business, selling sheet music and music books. Thompson turned out to have considerable business savvy. He marketed his music by sending copies to various minstrel shows, which were popular at the time - and he may have paid some of them to sing his music. He quickly became successful, and was known as the millionaire "Bard of Ohio". He wrote one of his most popular songs, "Gathering Sea Shells on the Sea Short", in ten minutes. It sold 246,000 copies. Thompson was a Christian, and while attending a Dwight L. Moody evangelistic meeting decided to devote himself to writing and promoting Christian music. He wrote "Softly and Tenderly Jesus is Calling" in 1880. It quickly became popular as a hymn of invitation in evangelistic meetings, and was included in church hymnals as well. Thompson wrote "Jesus is All the World to Me" in 1904, and it also became very popular. He was as successful with Christian music as he had been earlier with secular music. Dwight L. Moody, the most famous evangelist of his day, used "Softly and Tenderly" as an invitation hymn in his meetings. Thompson visited Moody as the latter was dying, and Moody told him, "Will, I would rather have written 'Softly and Tenderly Jesus is Calling' than anything I have been able to do in my life". Thompson continued to live a life of service and supported various civic and religious activities generously. He was also aware of the fact that small town people had very little exposure to good music, so he loaded a piano on a horse-drawn wagon and went through small Ohio towns giving concerts of his music. Thompson became ill on a trip to Europe in 1909, and died shortly after.

87 - GOD WILL TAKE CARE OF YOU

William Martin was a traveling evangelist in the early 1900s. On one occasion, he visited the Practical Bible Training School in New York, where he assisted the principal in putting together a songbook. One Sunday, he was scheduled to speak in a church a good distance from the school. As he was preparing to leave, his wife, Civilla, became quite ill, and Mr. Martin felt he should cancel his engagement. As the Martins discussed what to do, their nine year old son blurted out these words: "Oh, Daddy, you don't have to stay home because of mother. God will take care of us." William followed his son's words of encouragement and went on to the church service. Later that morning, he received word from his wife saying, "All is well. God did take care of us." The words of the Martins' son had a profound effect on Mrs. Martin's heart, and by the time Dr. Martin returned home, his wife had written a poem. When he came home, relieved to find his wife much better, she gave the words to him. He sat down at the organ and within an hour composed music to go with them. Later in the week, it was sung at a school assembly, and then it was added to a songbook. That poem, "God Will Take Care of You", would be recorded with Civilla

Martin as the author and with her husband as the composer. But, in reality, it was simple childlike faith that gave birth to the song that has supplied comfort for many years. One man in particular, about 25 years or so after it was written, was hospitalized with a severe case of shingles. Some of his business deals had failed, he was in physical as well as emotional pain, and filled with despair and little hope. One morning while in his hospital bed, he heard this hymn coming from the hospital chapel. The man followed the music into the chapel and as he listened, he felt his burdens lift. His worries left him as he realized just how much God loved him. He later recalled those moments in the chapel as some of the most glorious minutes of my life. Who was the man who was so filled with despair? Mr. James C. Penney, founder of the department store chain, J.C. Penney.

88 - TAKE THE NAME OF JESUS WITH YOU

So many of the great hymns were written by folks who lived with serious physical challenges. Lydia Baxter (1809-1874) was a bedridden invalid for much of her life, but that didn't keep her from leading a life full of service and encouragement. She and her sister participated in establishing a Baptist Church in Petersburg, New York. After her marriage, she and her husband moved to New York City, where her home became known as a gathering place for preachers, evangelists, and Christian workers who would come to her for inspiration and advice. Even as she was bedridden, folks who paid a visit to her sickroom were not so much comforting to her as they were encouraged in their own lives and spirits. Mrs. Baxter studied the Bible carefully and especially enjoyed learning the meaning of the names mentioned in the text. Of all the biblical names she knew, the name of Jesus meant the most to her. Whenever she was questioned about her cheery disposition, despite her physical limitations, she would reply, "I have a very special armor. I have the name of Jesus. When the tempter tries to make me blue or despondent, I mention the name of Jesus, and he can't get through to me anymore." The hymn, "Take the name of Jesus with you", was most likely written by her on her sickbed, four years before her death in 1874. William H. Doane composed the music for this text shortly after Mrs. Baxter wrote it, and the hymn was first published in the hymnal, "Pure Gold", in 1871. This hymn was frequently used during the Moody-Sankey evangelistic campaigns, toward the end of the nineteenth century. Although she wrote a number of other Gospel hymns, this is the only one that is still in wide use today. It has often been used in church services as a closing hymn since it provides an important reminder to go out each day, taking his name with us, while sharing with others what Jesus has done in our lives. In one sense the hymn is really the personal testimony of Lydia Baxter's experiences with the name of Jesus throughout her life.

89 - ALL THE WAY MY SAVIOR LEADS ME

"All the Way My Savior Leads Me" came from the grateful heart of the blind hymn writer, Fanny Crosby, after she had received a direct answer to prayer. The story is included in Crosby's autobiography: "The writing of this hymn, 'All the Way My Savior Leads Me', was the result of a personal experience. One day, I wanted the modestly substantial amount of five dollars for a particular purpose, and needed it very badly. I did not know, just then, exactly how to get it and was led to pray for it. Somehow I knew the good Lord would give it to me if I asked him for it. Not long after I had prayed for the money, a gentleman came into the house, passed the time of day, shook hands with me, and went out immediately. When I closed my hand, after the friendly salutation, I found in it a bill which he left there. A visitor later told me it was a five dollar bill. I have no way to account for this, except to believe that God, in answer to my prayer, put it into the heart of this good man to bring me the money. My first thought was, in what a wonderful way the Lord helps me! All the way my Savior leads me! I immediately wrote the hymn, and Dr. Robert Lowry, the famous preacher and hymn writer, set it to music."

90 - 'TIS SO SWEET TO TRUST IN JESUS

The stories behind many hymns are tragic, but they also confirm for us that God uses these tragedies as a way to bring blessing. The story behind "'Tis So Sweet to Trust in Jesus" is a good example of this. The author, Louisa Stead, suffered tragedy and hardship, but out of these struggles came blessing to many for years afterwards. Two experiences in particular in her life demonstrated to Louisa the importance of trusting in Jesus. Louisa Stead was born in Dover, England in 1850. She married in 1875 and moved to the US, where the couple had a daughter, Lily. When Lily was four years old, the family went out to enjoy a picnic lunch one day at the beach on Long Island, New York. As they were sitting on the ground, they suddenly heard cries for help and spotted a boy struggling in the sea. Mr. Stead charged into the water after the boy but was pulled under by the panicked youngster, and both of them drowned before the terrified eyes of Louisa and her daughter. Out of her pain and hardship, and as she tried to come to grips with this tragedy, Louisa held on to her trust in God. No longer with a husband or income, Louisa and her daughter were reduced to such poverty that it was not uncommon for them to have no food left in the house. On one such occasion, Louisa's prayer to the Lord for provision was answered inexplicably the next morning when she found a basket of groceries and money on her doorstep. It was during these life struggles that Louisa wrote the hymn, "'Tis So Sweet to Trust in Jesus". Sometime later, Louisa and Lily left for South Africa, where Louisa worked as a missionary for 15 years. Louisa passed away after a long illness in 1917. Following her death, Christians in Rhodesia noted that: "We miss her very much, but her influence goes on as our 5,000 converts continually sing this hymn in their native language."

91 - HAVE THINE OWN WAY, LORD

This hymn was inspired by a simple prayer of an elderly woman at a prayer meeting, when she spoke these words: "It really doesn't matter what you do with us, Lord - just have your way with our lives..." The author of the hymn was Adelaide Pollard, who was born in Iowa in 1862. After her education, she moved to Chicago to became a teacher. She also taught Bible studies. At the same time, Miss Pollard wanted very much to be a missionary in Africa, as her heart's burden was for the lost. When this plan did not materialize, she taught at a Missionary Training School. She did finally make it to Africa for a brief time before World War I, but she had to spend the war years in Scotland. After returning to the United States, she continued her ministry even though she was in poor health. "Have Thine Own Way, Lord" was composed during a time when Miss Pollard was trying to raise funds to make a trip to Africa. However, being unsuccessful at this effort left her feeling distressed and wondering what God's will was. She paused at one point to ask herself, "Why is this so hard?" If God really wanted her to go to Africa at the age of 40, shouldn't it be easier? Should he not be easing the way, instead of making it so difficult? These are some of the questions that came to her mind and were also being asked by her friends and family. One day she went to church to spend some time in prayer. As she prayed, an elderly lady came up beside her, and knowing the burden of her heart, prayed this way: "Lord, it doesn't matter what you bring into our lives. Just have your way with us." This prayer brought a moment of clarity for Adelaide. She went home, sat down, and wrote the lyrics to the hymn as they began to take shape in her mind.

92 - JESUS PAID IT ALL

On a Sunday morning in 1865, Elvina Hall was in her usual seat in the church choir. But as the words of the Reverend Schrick's prayer went on and on, her thoughts began to wander elsewhere. She pondered the meaning of the cross, and the well known scene came to her mind. As the pastor's prayer continued, Mrs. Hall reached for her hymnbook and, turning to the inside cover, began to write down her thoughts. After the service, she presented the pastor with the poetry she had just put together. Looking at the words, the pastor remembered something that had happened that same week. The church organist had composed a hymn tune and given it to Pastor Schrick, suggesting they might be able to use it in the future. Stepping into his study, the pastor now laid Mrs. Hall's poem next to the lines of music. To his surprise, he realized that they fit together perfectly. "Indeed, God works in mysterious ways!", he thought. The words and tune have been sung together ever since in the hymn, "Jesus Paid It All".

93 - A CHILD OF THE KING

Harriett Buell was born in 1834 in Cazevia, New York. Buell wrote this song one Sunday morning while walking home from her church. She then sent the text to the Northern Christian Advocate, and they printed it. The poem was titled "The Child of a King". At the same time, John Sumner had been praying for a Gospel song to write which would replace the one his friend, Philip Bliss, had promised to write before his unexpected death. John Sumner served as a minister in Pennsylvania and New York, as well as being a music teacher. When Sumner saw Mrs. Buell's words in publication, he knew his prayer had been answered. He set a melody to the poem. Peter Bilhorn tells the following story from 1883: "We had started up the Missouri River for Bismarck, and on Sunday we stopped at a town, named Blunt, to unload some freight. A crowd of men and boys came down to the wharf. I took my little organ, went on the wharf-boat, and sang a few songs - among others the glorious hymn, 'I'm a child of the King'. I thought nothing more of the occasion until long afterward, when I sang the same song in Dwight L. Moody's church in Chicago. Then a man in the back part of the house arose, and said in a trembling voice: 'Two years ago I heard that song at Blunt, Dakota; I was then an unsaved man, but that song set me to thinking, and I decided to accept Christ, and I am now studying for the ministry.'"

God's ways are mysterious and amazing!

94 - LEANING ON THE EVERLASTING ARMS

Anthony Showalter studied music in England, France, and Germany. He also taught music, and published over 130 music books. One day the postman delivered letters to him from two of his former students. Each letter brought the tragic news that the man's wife had died, both on the same day. Showalter responded to each man, giving encouragement and comfort as he was able. He included Deuteronomy 33:27 in his letters: "The eternal God is your refuge, and underneath are the everlasting arms." Mr. Showalter recounted later, "Before completing the writing of the sentence, the thought came to me that the fact that we may lean on those everlasting arms and find comfort and strength ought to be put into a song. And before finishing the letter, the words and music of the refrain were written." He then sent his newly composed music to his friend, the hymn writer, Elisha Hoffman, who then came up with three stanzas to match. Out of the kind comfort sent to the widowed men the hymn, "Leaning on the Everlasting Arms", was born.

95 - I NEED THEE EVERY HOUR

Annie Hawks was born in Hoosick, New York, in 1835. At an early age she was already writing poetry and, when she was 14, she had some of her work published in a newspaper. When she married at 24, Annie moved to Brooklyn, New York. She and her husband joined a church whose pastor was Robert Lowry, known for his hymn writing and composing as well as being the pastor. Lowry immediately recognized Mrs. Hawks' talent for writing and encouraged her to use it. He even offered her a challenge: "If you'll write the words", he said, "I'll write the music", and he did exactly that. Mrs. Hawks wrote "I Need Thee Every Hour" in 1872. It was most likely based on the words of Jesus in John 15:4-5: "Abide in me, and I in you. As the branch cannot bear fruit of itself, except it abide in the vine; no more can ye, except ye abide in me. I am the vine, ye are the branches: he that abideth in me, I am in him, the same bringeth forth much fruit: for without me ye can do nothing." The new hymn was performed that year at the National Sunday School Convention in Cincinatti, Ohio. Soon after that it was introduced by the evangelistic team of Moody and Sankey, who, most likely, did much to make it popular. It was translated into many other languages and was even featured in the Chicago World's Fair.

Shortly before her death in 1918, Mrs. Hawkes gave the full background story behind the hymn: "I remember well the circumstances under which I wrote the hymn. It was a bright June day, and I became so filled with the sense of the nearness of my Master that I began to wonder how anyone could live without Him, in either joy or pain. Suddenly, the words "I need Thee every hour", flashed into my mind, and very quickly the thought had full possession of me. Seating myself by the open windows, I caught up my pencil and committed the words to paper - almost as they are today. A few months later Dr. Robert Lowry composed the tune needed for my hymn and also added the refrain. For myself, the hymn, at its writing, was prophetic rather than expressive of my own experiences, for it was wafted out to the world on the wings of love and joy, instead of under the stress of great personal sorrow, with which it has often been associated. At first I did not understand why the hymn so greatly touched the throbbing heart of humanity. Years later, however, under the shadow of a great loss, I came to understand something of the comforting power of the words I had been permitted to give out to others in my hours of sweet serenity and peace." Regarding the loss she said that she experienced later in life, her husband died in Brooklyn in 1888 at age 55. Additionally, the couple had three children, only one of whom was still living in 1893.

96 - REVIVE US AGAIN

"Revive Us Again" was written by William MacKay, a medical doctor in Scotland. He was born in 1839 and, at the age of 17, left home to study medicine at the University of Edinburgh. William's mother gave him a Bible and wrote his name and a verse of Scripture in it. Although he began his studies well, as time went by he drifted away from his Christian upbringing and began drinking heavily. At a particularly low point in his life, to purchase some whiskey, MacKay pawned away the Bible his mother had given him. After graduating from medical school, his first assignment was in a hospital emergency room. While working there, Dr. MacKay became acquainted with human suffering. Occasionally, the doctor would witness the remarkable difference in the life of a person who had faith in Jesus Christ. Dr. MacKay did not think it was strange to see the difference in a Christian because he had been raised in a godly home. His mother had led him to Christ as a young man and prayed often for her son. One day a young construction worker was brought into the emergency room. He had fallen off a scaffold and was in critical condition. William worked on the young man, but it quickly became clear that because of his serious injuries, his case was hopeless. All William could do was relieve the young man's pain as much as possible. Dr. MacKay asked the young man, "Do you have any relatives that we can notify of your injuries?" The young man replied, "No sir. I live alone in this world. However, would you please notify my landlady and ask her to come visit me. I owe her some money and want to pay her. Also when she comes, ask her to bring me my book." "What book?" Dr. MacKay asked. "Oh just tell her to bring the book. She will know what book I am talking about," the patient responded. Dr. MacKay checked on him several times a day while he was in the emergency room. He noticed a calm expression on the young man's face when he talked with him. MacKay guessed that the young man was a Christian, but he did not want to talk about that with him or anyone else. The landlady brought the young man his Bible, and he read it constantly. When he could not read it any longer, he just laid his Bible on his chest and hugged it. After about a week the young man died. Afterwards, Dr. MacKay was called to his room by the nurses to fill out some necessary paperwork, and one of the nurses asked the doctor, "What should I do with this Bible?" Dr. MacKay told the nurse that the young man had no relatives, and that she could just give him the Bible and he would get rid of it. While the nurses tended to the body of the young man, Dr. Mackay opened up the front of the Bible and curiously looked at the first few pages. Suddenly, he slammed the Bible closed with a strange look on his face. A nurse noticed Dr.

MacKay's countenance and asked, "Are you alright?" MacKay answered, "Yes, I am going to my office; if you need me you can call me there." He went to his office and shut the door, sat at his desk, and opened the Bible once again. There it was – his mother's own handwriting. The Bible was inscribed by his mother and was the very Bible that Dr. MacKay's mother had given him as he left home for medical school. The young man must have bought the Bible from the pawn shop where the doctor pawned it for drinking money. All the pages were well worn and some pages were loose. Many verses had been underlined. Dr. MacKay thought about how his Bible had brought comfort to this dying young man. It was the book that enabled him to die in peace and happiness. With a sense of shame, Dr. MacKay began to read some of the Bible verses that were underlined. He recounted: "Many verses I had heard in my younger years came back to me. The voice in my conscience could not be silenced any longer. With tears in my eyes, I prayed for God to forgive me and restore to me the joy of my salvation". It was not long after Dr. MacKay's Bible miraculously came back to him that he wrote the words for the hymn, "Revive Us Again". He was most certainly thinking about this incident as he penned the words, "may each soul be rekindled with fire from above". It was the return of his Bible that brought revival to his own heart. He quit the medical profession, entered theological college and became a pastor of a church in Scotland. He wrote 17 other hymns, but this is the only one still in use today.

97 - HE WILL HOLD ME FAST

While in Toronto in 1906, Robert Harkness had a conversation with a young believer who was struggling with the worry of staying faithful to Christ in the future. Later that day, Harkness wrote a letter to hymn writer Ada Habershon about the need for a song which would give assurance of faithfulness in our Christian walk. Shortly afterwards, she sent back lyrics to seven different songs. One of them was "He Will Hold Me Fast". Harkness wrote music for the hymn during church one morning, and about 4,000 people sang it that evening. Ada Habershon was born in 1861 in Marylebone, England. Soon after she began to write hymns, R. A. Torrey and Charles Alexander asked Ada to write some selections for their evangelistic tour in 1905. In "Torrey and Alexander: The Story of a World-Wide Revival", Robert Harkness shared about being in Philadelphia in 1906. He said, "I remember Dr. Torrey was preaching to several thousand people. During a sermon I took out some slips of paper with words which Miss Habershon had sent over in response to a request for some verses about keeping the power of Christ. I read over the lines of 'He will hold me fast'; the melody came to me, and

I worked it out there and then, writing the music for the verses and the chorus." At a Moody Bible Conference in 1907, the song was described as having "captivated everybody...and was sung and whistled all over the grounds". The song has many testimonies from people stating it was "just what I need" to "electrifying the crowd". The song is an amazing reminder that we have our hope and eternal security in a God who will not let us go. The love of Christ, evidenced by His sacrifice, assures us of this hope and truth. Regardless of what we've done or what we will do, Christ will hold us fast. There is nothing that can be done to pull His love from us. In 1908, Charles Alexander shared this testimony in relation to the impact of the song: "During our mission in Philadelphia last spring, Dr. Charles Gordon called me across the waiting room of the hotel where we were staying and introduced me to a young man, and told me his story. His face was shining as he told us how he had been in our meeting a few days before and had been converted. When I questioned him I found that he had been in darkness, and felt he was too weak to live a Christian life. He was in the meeting when I was leading the people in the song, 'He will hold me fast', and he said that was the very message he needed. The thought that Christ could hold him fast, and that he need not depend upon his own will power, or his own strength, was the means of his decision for Christ." A few weeks after the Philadelphia crusade, Chapman and

Alexander were leading a crusade in Kansas City. A reporter described how "He will hold me fast" was a highlight of the experience: "The climax of the service of song came when Mr. Alexander united choir and audience - 6,000 strong - in singing Mr. Harkness' new hymn, 'He will hold me fast'."

98 - LOVE LIFTED ME

"Love Lifted Me" was a joint effort by James Rowe and Howard E. Smith. Rowe was born in England in 1865. He was the son of a copper miner. James worked for the Irish government for four years before immigrating to America. He settled in Albany, NY and went to work on the railroad for the next ten years. Later, he was employed by music publishers in Texas and Tennessee. James Rowe became a full time writer who composed hymns and edited music journals. Rowe and Smith wrote several hymns together. Howard E. Smith, born in 1863, suffered from arthritis which caused his hands to be terribly twisted. According to Rowe's daughter, Smith's hands had become knotted with arthritis, but he could still play the piano. "Love Lifted Me" was written in 1912. Rowe and Smith wrote the hymn based on the passage in Matthew 14 of Peter walking on the water, becoming afraid, and crying out to the Lord to save him as he was sinking. Matthew 8 is also referred to in the hymn. As the hymn developed, Smith would play a few notes and jot them down, matching them with the words Rowe was writing as they went along. Rowe's daughter shared what she remembered about the occasion: "I can see them now, my father striding up and down humming a bar or two, and Howard playing it and jotting it down… The two huddled together, working line by line, composing this hymn in tandem." Rowe reminds us of the "redemption from sin by our Saviour" in the first verse of this hymn. The second verse shows "the change in our walk as we owe Him our song, our service, our whole heart". The last verse is a witness to the lost.

99 - LEAD ON, O KING ETERNAL

Just as Ernest Shurtleff was about to graduate from Andover Seminary in 1887, his classmates came to him asking if he would come up with a poem especially for their class. Shurtleff decided it would be a good opportunity to create a hymn that conveyed their preparation at seminary and the tasks that were to follow as they went out into the world. Although the expressions in the hymn were intended to challenge that graduating class at the seminary, the truths conveyed have been used to speak to many succeeding generations about our spiritual pilgrimage in a fallen world. He wrote "Lead on, O King Eternal" for that occasion. This hymn is really a prayer for God's guidance. It speaks of marching, "fields of conquest", and "battle song" — not because it celebrates war, but because it acknowledges the daily struggle in which good people must engage against evil. It looks forward to the celebration of victory — not with swords and drums, but with "deeds of love and mercy" — recognizing that Christ calls us to conquer the world by demonstrating love and mercy rather than by using force. This hymn expresses the difficulties of the Christian life — as we stand armed only with holiness against "sin's fierce war". It acknowledges the reality of the cross, but celebrates the reality of the crown — the reward of those who are faithful — and closes, "Lead on, O God of might!" It was the only hymn Shurtleff produced. He went on to serve as a pastor, and he and his wife did relief work in Europe during World War I. He died in France at the age of fifty-five. Before studying at Andover, Ernest Shurtleff attended Harvard University. He served Congregational churches in California, Massachusetts, and Minnesota before moving to Europe. In 1905 he established the American Church in Frankfurt, and in 1906 he moved to Paris, where he was involved in student ministry at the Academy Vitti. During World War I, he and his wife were active in refugee relief work in Paris. During an influenza epidemic, he died at Paris on August 24, 1917.

100 - FAITH OF OUR FATHERS

Raised in the Church of England, Frederick W. Faber was born in Yorkshire, England, 1814 and died in London in 1863. He came from a Huguenot and Calvinistic family, was educated at Oxford University, and ordained in the Church of England in 1839. However, he was influenced by the teaching of John Henry Newman, and Faber followed Newman into the Roman Catholic Church in 1845 and served under Newman's supervision. Because he believed that Roman Catholics should sing hymns like those written by John Newton, Charles Wesley, and William Cowper, Faber wrote 150 hymns himself. This hymn was written by Faber in 1849. He wrote several hymns and articles defending teachings and honoring the Catholic faithful. The hymn "Faith of our Fathers" was penned to honor the memory of Catholic martyrs who were persecuted by the Church of England during the time of turmoil. The composition originally was written in honor of Catherine of Alexander, a fourth-century woman put to death because of her faith. The faith of our fathers referred to in this hymn is their abundant trust in the loving, Heavenly Father who we learn about in the Scriptures.

101 - JOYFUL, JOYFUL, WE ADORE THEE

Written in 1907 and based on Psalm 71, the hymn, "Joyful, Joyful, We Adore Thee", was composed by Henry van Dyke. He was born in Germantown, Pennsylvania, in 1852 and was a Presbyterian minister for 27 years and a well known worship leader at the time. Van Dyke also served as a professor of literature at Princeton University for 23 years, was the moderator of his Presbyterian denomination, became a Navy chaplain during World War 1, and represented his country as an ambassador to Holland and Luxembourg under Woodrow Wilson. He wrote over 70 devotional and other books, and some became bestsellers. This is the best known of van Dyke's hymns. About this hymn, he explained: "These verses are simple expressions of common Christian feelings and desires that may be sung together by people who are not afraid that any truth of science will destroy their religion or that any revolution on earth will overthrow the kingdom of heaven. Therefore these are hymns of trust and hope." "Joyful, Joyful, We Adore Thee", was given to the President of Williams College in Massachusetts during a graduation ceremony when van Dyke was the guest speaker. Inspired by the beauty and greatness of the Berkshire Mountains, he suggested the text be sung to Beethoven's "Hymn to Joy". Van Dyke described the hymn as one of love, hope, and the trust in God's providence over nature and us. The poem portrays the connection between God and his creation and expresses how that connection brings us joy. Henry van Dyke was staying at the home of the president of the college and woke up one morning, looked out at the mountains and, in awe of God's great creation, wrote the words to "Joyful, Joyful, We Adore Thee". Van Dyke was also the author of the Christmas story, "The Other Wise Man", and wrote several books of poetry. But of all his writings he is best remembered for this hymn, "Joyful, Joyful, We Adore Thee".

102 - PRAISE, MY SOUL, THE KING OF HEAVEN

Henry Francis Lyte, the author of this hymn, didn't have an easy life. His father abandoned the family while Henry was still a boy. Then Henry's mother and brother died, leaving Henry an orphan at age nine. Thankfully, a Christian couple took him in and provided for his education. Lyte studied for the ministry, was ordained, and served several small churches - the last in Brixham on the English Channel - a fishing village where he served for 23 years. While there, he formed a Sunday school that enrolled about 800 children. Lyte also wrote many hymns based on the Psalms. "Praise, My Soul, the King of Heaven," based on Psalm 103, is one of those. Queen Elizabeth had it sung as the processional for her coronation. Another of Lyte's hymns, "Abide with me", was the favorite hymn of King George V. Lyte was in bad health for most of his life, and died at age 54. He had never been anything but a village pastor, but he enriched the lives of those in his community and the sailors to whom he carried on a special ministry - and all of us who continue to enjoy his hymns. I suspect that no one would have been more surprised than Henry Lyte to learn that one of his hymns was the favorite of the King and another was sung at Queen Elizabeth's wedding, as well as at her coronation. But that is often how God works - using people who we might think of as being ordinary to give us extraordinary blessings. Born in Scotland in 1793, Henry Francis Lyte was educated at Trinity College, Dublin, where he distinguished himself by winning the English prize poem three times. Originally intending to study medicine, he abandoned the sciences for theology. In 1817, he moved to Cornwall. There, he underwent a spiritual change, which shaped and influenced the rest of his life, the immediate cause being the illness and death of a brother clergyman. Lyte said of him: "He died happy under the belief that though he had deeply erred, there was One whose death and sufferings would atone for his delinquencies, and be accepted for all that he had incurred." He added, "I was greatly affected by the matter, and brought to look at life and its issue with a different eye than before; and I began to study my Bible, and preach in another manner than I had previously done." In 1823, he was appointed as a pastor in Devon. He composed his "Tales on the Lord's Prayer" in 1826 and remained in Devon until his death in 1847.

103 - ALL CREATURES OF OUR GOD AND KING

Giovanni di Bernadone, better known as Francis of Assisi, was born in 1181 into a family of seven children, during the time of the Crusades, when the upper class ruled the land and armored knights rode on their horses across the European countryside. Francis enjoyed living in a wealthy family, and as a child he took advantage of the decadent life his family was able to afford by engaging in mischief with his friends. After a youth spent in indulgence, he became a soldier and at age 20, fought in a battle, and was captured and imprisoned for a year or more. A serious illness in 1202 brought about a change in his life, and at age 25 he decided to serve God by imitating the selfless life of Christ. He longed for greater intimacy with Christ and decided to give up his wealth and follow Jesus fully, taking a vow before God to live in poverty. His life was spent in prayer, poverty, and caring for the needs of others. Francis' exuberant joy in living for Jesus in such a simple way resulted in his father disowning him. He spent a life of wandering through the valleys and hills of Italy, singing as he went. Barefoot and dressed in rough clothing, Francis lived among the poor and lepers and shared the love of Jesus. Over time, young men were inspired by his way of life and joined him in sleeping in barns, church porches, and makeshift shelters, ministering to the sick and poor and enjoying God's creation around them. One writer described Francis' unique perspective in this way: "Working among the lepers as well as society's rejected became a joy for Francis as he realized that tending to them was the ministry he had received from Christ through the Gospel. For Francis, Christians do not attain heights of glory through seclusion or attending to our own needs; rather, we meet God in the fullness of his glory as we attend to others in their need." A hymn of praise to God that was written by Francis seems to be paraphrased from Psalm 145 is "All Creatures Of Our God And King".

104 - I HEARD THE VOICE OF JESUS SAY

Horatius Bonar was born in 1808 in Edinburgh, where his family belonged to the Church of Scotland. Bonar entered the ministry and became a pastor in the rural town of Kelso. Bonar also began writing hymns. After the turbulence and disruption of the Church of Scotland in 1843 he became a Free Church of Scotland minister. Bonar also wrote evangelical tracts, and had a great ministry among children. He published "God's Way of Peace: a Book for the Anxious", which was translated into three languages and sold over a quarter of a million copies in his lifetime. Ironically, he never heard his own hymns sung in his church in Edinburgh, as his was one of the Free Church congregations that opposed the use of hymns in worship services! "I heard the voice of Jesus say" (based on Matthew 11: 28) was written in 1846, during an intensely stressful and painful time just after the 1843 church division. Bonar spent the next 20 years pastoring the congregation in Kelso, writing, and engaging in evangelism. Throughout his life he had been strongly influenced by Thomas Chalmers, and in 1866 he planted a new church in Edinburgh called the Chalmers Memorial Chapel. He served that church until just before his death. Bonar had begun to write hymns before his ordination when he was serving as superintendent of a Sunday school. He realized that the children didn't love or appreciate the songs they had been singing, so he set out to write a few hymns with simpler lyrics and already familiar tunes. These hymns were received wonderfully. It wasn't long after this that Bonar, having a gift and an interest in writing spiritual poems, began writing adult hymns. In the course of his ministry he published a number of hymn compilations. "I Heard the Voice of Jesus Say" was one of the hymns he wrote during his time at Kelso and is probably his most famous song, having been well received all across the English-speaking world. What makes the hymn so widely appealing is its focus on the Gospel call of Christ to come to him, look to him, drink, and rest, and the call to obey and to find in him all that he has promised. It is simple, sweet, and encouraging. As with most of his hymns, Rev. Bonar wrote this one with children in mind, being concerned that they learn and sing the great truths about Christ. Perhaps his love of children came from the fact that he and his wife lost five of their own in rapid succession. While many of his hymns were originally written for children, they were so full of sound teaching that adults loved to sing them as well.

105 - LET US WITH A GLADSOME MIND

"Let us with a gladsome mind" was written in 1623 by John Milton (1608-1674), the famous author of "Paradise Lost". Milton was an English poet and debater, and served the Commonwealth of England under Oliver Cromwell. He is best known for his epic "Paradise Lost", and he left a strong influence on poetry and other literature. Milton based "Let us with a gladsome mind" on Psalm 136. Remarkably, he wrote the hymn at age 15. Apparently he hadn't intended to write a hymn, and the poem was only set to music after Milton's death. His grandfather had converted from Catholicism to Protestantism, and his father had been disinherited during Queen Elizabeth's reign for reading the Bible. The singing of Psalms from the Old Testament was the almost universal form of music in English churches from about 1550 to nearly 1700. However, some began to feel that the current Psalters had departed too much from the sense of the Hebrew text, while others believed that David's Psalms did not really convey the true Christian life. So the Anglican Church began turning to the use of hymns. Milton, who became one of the finest representatives of this aspect of 17th century Puritanism, was educated at St. Paul's School in London. While living at home, Milton produced this poem from Psalm 136, evidently for his own pleasure and as well as for his father and teachers. It was natural, considering his Puritan heritage, that he would turn to the Bible for his inspiration. Milton was imitating his elders, but many feel that he did a better job than they did. The poem, "Let us with a gladsome mind", was not published until 1645 in his "Poems, Both English and Latin". When he was 16, Milton entered Christ College at Cambridge. After receiving his master's degree, he studied full time while he lived with his parents at Horton for six years and then travelled across Europe. He then settled in Aldersgate and opened a school for a few years. In 1643 Milton married; however, his wife, Mary, died ten years later, and at the same time, he became totally blind. Later he married Katherine Woodcock and, after her death, Elizabeth Minshull. During the years of Oliver Cromwell, from 1649 to 1659 he served as secretary of foreign affairs until the return of the monarchy. His fame came from his prose written during the years of the Commonwealth, in which he sought to justify Puritanism, and most of all the great English epic poems during the latter part of his life, including "Paradise Lost" and "Paradise Regained". He died in St. Giles in 1674. The poem was never used as a hymn until 1855, when it was included in the "Congregationalist Hymn Book". His poem "Paradise Lost" is known as one of the greatest works of literature in history, and he is regarded by some as one of the greatest English writers in history.

106 - IF THOU BUT SUFFER GOD TO GUIDE THEE

The writer of this hymn, Georg Neumark (1621–81), experienced some extremely difficult moments in his life. At that time in Europe, social and economic conditions were deplorable, the bloody Thirty Years' War was in progress (1618–48), and he personally lost everything. Neumark joined a group going from Leipzig to Lübeck, in Germany, planning to travel to Königsberg to attend university there. But along the way, they were attacked by bandits, who robbed Neumark of everything except his prayer book and a little money sewed up in his clothes. But now without funds to pursue his education, Neumark was forced to look for a job. He went from town to town, but was unable to find work. Walking the countryside with an uncertain and bleak future, he was rescued when the Lord brought Nicholas Becker into his life. Pastor Becker, after learning of his desperation, was able to arrange for Neumark to become a tutor for a family in Kiel. Then in 1646 he again lost all his belongings in a fire. The tutorial work provided Neumark with some stability and steady employment. It was at this time that Neumark composed this hymn. The words convey great hope and encouragement, and it quickly found its way into hymnals across Germany. But it may have been forgotten except for a British translator who had a special interest in German hymns. She translated hundreds of hymns into English, including "If Thou But Suffer God to Guide Thee". The hymn reminds us to walk in faith through even the most difficult times, knowing that God is guiding and will redeem our most difficult experiences for his good purposes. The road that led Neumark to pen this hymn came with the robbery he endured, his struggle to find work, and life generally not going according to plan, which was the case for a number of hymn-writers in that time period. In 1681, he went blind, but was permitted to keep his employment until he died. Despite his personal suffering, Neumark wrote many hymns in which he expressed his absolute trust in God.

107 - AND CAN IT BE THAT I SHOULD GAIN

Charles Wesley, who, along with his brother John, founded Methodism, was ordained in the Church of England in 1735. However, three years later, as he was studying his Bible, he wrote: "At midnight I gave myself to Christ, assured that I was safe, whether sleeping or waking. I had the continual experience of His power to overcome all temptation, and I confessed with joy and surprise that He was able to do exceedingly abundantly for me above what I can ask or think." Wesley was raised in a Christian home but had not yet been certain of his own salvation. He recorded in his journal: "I now found myself at peace with God, and rejoiced in hope of loving Christ. I saw that by faith I stood." Two days later, his noted in his journal that he had begun writing a hymn. This hymn was likely "And Can It Be" because of the vivid testimony it contains. It was one of the first of the more than 6,000 hymns he wrote. He began the first stanza by expressing admiration at the love Jesus demonstrated by dying for him. Three days before, his brother John experienced his heart "strangely warmed", and Charles was recovering from an illness when he heard a voice saying, "In the name of Jesus of Nazareth, arise, and believe, and thou shalt be healed of all thy infirmities". Charles got out of bed, picked up his Bible, and read in the Psalms: "He has put a new song in my mouth, even praise unto our God", as well as in Isaiah 40, "Comfort ye, comfort ye my people, saith your God". Moved and convicted, Charles reflected on these words until he was certain in his faith, recognizing that it is by faith we are saved (Ephesians 2:8). "And Can It Be" remains one of his most remarkable hymns, expressing the joy of receiving salvation. Wesley opens with an exclamation, "And can it be that I should gain an interest in my Savior's blood!" These words are followed by a question, "Died he for me — who caused his pain?" Both are typical of Charles' poetic style and imagery.

108 - THERE IS A GREEN HILL FAR AWAY

Cecil Frances Alexander, one of the best known women hymn writers, was born in Tyrone, Ireland. As a small girl, Cecil Frances (1818-1895) wrote poetry in her school journal. While teaching Sunday School, she loved to convey to the children spiritual truths through the use of hymns. In 1848 she published a volume of children's hymns that covered a wide range of biblical subjects such as baptism, the Lord's Supper, the Ten Commandments, and prayer, writing in simple language for children. She wrote over 200 hymns which attempted to "make theology picturesque"; she also wrote poems, many of which were biblically-based. Almost all of the 400 poems and hymns that were written by Mrs. Alexander were intended for children. The language she used is direct and easily understood, as it is in this hymn, and this beautiful text explains simply the story of Christ's redemption. Mrs. Alexander wanted to teach her Sunday School class the meaning of "suffered under Pontius Pilate, was crucified, dead and buried" from the Apostles' Creed. This hymn has also been greatly used by Christians in congregations for over a century. After she married Rev. Alexander, she was involved in helping him in his parish duties as well as in works of charity. She showed her concern by visiting the sick and the poor, providing them with food, clothes, and medical supplies. Her husband wrote this tribute about her: "From one poor home to another she went. Christ was ever with her, and in her, and all felt her influence." Those who knew her said that her life was even more beautiful than her hymns and poetry. "There is a green hill far away" talks about the death of Jesus. Penned while sitting beside the bed of a sick child, it was written in response to the remark of one of her godsons that he couldn't understand the Catechism. it was first published in her "Hymns for Little Children". Although she had never seen the rocky, barren hills outside Jerusalem, she used to imagine the location of Jesus' death as being like a little grassy hill by the road in Derry, Ireland. With her great passion for children, Cecil gave the proceeds from her book toward a school for deaf and mute children, which she started and which initially met on her family's property. Her concern for the interests of children shows in the way her hymns use simple language in simple phrases. One writer noticed her skill in this area and remarked: "Mrs. Alexander was always in touch with the thoughts and feelings of children, and she surpassed all other writers of sacred song in meeting a growing demand for children's hymns - hymns attractive in their simplicity, picturesqueness, and pathos, and yet without blemish in hymnic beauty." Her work was also born out of a personal commitment to Christ-like service toward others. Upon her death, the local rector noted how the older people of his parish recalled her charitable work: "The parish clerk still remembers her carrying soup and other nourishment to the sick and poor in the remote parts of the parish and in the most inclement weather, and often has seen her returning from her ministrations of loving and practical sympathy wet through. She sent a man to school whose education had been neglected in his youth, and gave him a weekly allowance out of her own purse, and when he had made sufficient progress Mrs. Alexander procured an appointment for him as national school teacher. As beautifully put in her exquisite hymn, 'There is a green hill far away', she trusted in His redeeming blood, and tried his works to do." Her husband believed that "There is a green hill far away" was among her best hymns, and he was always proud to be known as the husband of the great hymn writer. This hymn was also sung at his graveside.

109 - THINE IS THE GLORY

A song which emphasizes the victory of Christ over the grave is "Thine Is The Glory". The hymn was written by Edmond Louis Budry, who was born in 1854, at Vevay, Switzerland, on the shore of Lake Geneva, an ancient town mentioned by the writer Ptolemy in the Second Century. After studying theology, Budry served as a minister near Lausanne from 1881 to 1889, before returning to minister in the Free Church in Vevey, where he remained for 35 years. Writing "A toi la gloire" (to you the glory) in 1884, Budry probably never would have imagined that his hymn would become one of the best known in the world. Budry wrote over 60 chorales and also translated hymns from German, English, and Latin. "Thine is the glory" and some of his other works appeared in 1885 in "Chants Evangeliques" published in Lausanne. It would be 20 years before the hymn became well known by being published in the YMCA Hymnbook in 1904, and 20 more years before it became known to English-speakers, when it was translated into English in 1923, the year Budry retired. "Thine is the glory" may have been less popular without the music it was sung to, which was composed in 1747 by George Frederick

Handel, and which Budry fit the words to. The hymn has strong theology, is rooted in Scripture, and was inspired by the stories of Jesus rising from the dead. Frequently sung as an Easter hymn, it was perhaps written after the passing of Budry's wife, Marie. The text speaks of a war hero returning home victorious: our Lord and Savior Jesus Christ, who conquered death once and for all when he rose from the dead and paid the price for our sins. In 1933 the Methodist Hymn Book was the first in Europe to include the song, and hymnologist Fred Gaely adds that, "Budry was often asked to make translations of favorite German or English hymns, but he preferred to rewrite the texts, attempting to improve on the original, and often freely adapting old Latin hymns." John Wesley, a contemporary of Handel, enjoyed this tune very much and called it one of his favorites in his journal. In addition to the Gospel accounts of the resurrection, the text is also connected to Paul's words in I Corinthians 15:57: "But thanks be to God, which giveth us the victory through our Lord Jesus Christ."

110 - HE LEADETH ME

Joseph Gilmore was born in Boston in 1834 and studied at Brown University and Newton Theological Seminary. After his graduation, he taught Hebrew, served as a preacher at various churches, was a secretary to his father (the governor of New Hampshire), and also was the editor of the "Daily Monitor" in Concord. Gilmore then accepted the position as professor of logic, rhetoric, and English literature at the University of Rochester, where he taught until he retired in 1911. In addition to writing hymns on the side, Joseph produced academic books of art and literature. Hymnologist Williams Reynolds described Joseph as a man who was loved and respected in both religious and educational circles. But Christians remember him for one hymn, the story of which he shared as follows: "As a young man recently graduated, I was supplying for a couple of Sundays the pulpit of the First Baptist Church in Philadelphia. At the service, on the 26th of March, 1862, I set out to give the people an exposition of the Twenty-third Psalm, but I did not get further than the words 'He Leadeth Me'. Those words took hold of me as they had never done before, and I saw them in a significance and wondrous beauty of which I had never dreamed. It was the darkest hour of the Civil War. It may subconsciously have led me to realize that God's leadership is the one significant fact in human experience, that it makes no difference how we are led, or whither we are led, so long as we are sure God is leading us. At the close of the meeting a few of us kept on talking about the thought which I had emphasized; and then, on a blank page, I penciled the hymn, talking and writing at the same time, then handed it to my wife and thought no more about it. She sent it to The Watchman and Reflector, a paper published in Boston, where it was first printed. I did not know until 1865 that my hymn had been set to music by William B. Bradbury. I went to Rochester to preach as a candidate before the Second Baptist Church. Upon entering the chapel I took up a hymnal, thinking - I wonder what they sing here. To my amazement the book opened to 'He Leadeth Me', and that was the first time I knew that my hurriedly written lines had found a place among the songs of the church."

111 - GREAT IS THY FAITHFULNESS

Thomas Chisholm was born in 1866 in a log cabin in Franklin, Kentucky. He received his education in a rural schoolhouse in the area, but as poor as they were, he never got more than an elementary school education. However, by the age of 16 he was a teacher. Five years later, at the age of 21, he was the associate editor of his hometown weekly newspaper, The Franklin Advocate. In 1893, Henry Morrison, the founder of Asbury College and Seminary in Wilmore, Kentucky, held a revival meeting in Franklin. Chisholm attended and accepted Jesus Christ into his heart and life. Later, Morrison invited Thomas Chisholm to move to Louisville, Kentucky and became an editor for the Pentecostal Herald. In 1903, Chisholm became a Methodist minister. He also married Katherine Vandevere. Due to ill health, Chisholm was only able to serve one year in the ministry. Afterwards, he and his wife relocated to Indiana for the open air and later moved to New Jersey where he sold insurance. He suffered from health issues the rest of his life and sometimes was confined to his bed and unable to work. Thomas was good friends with William Runyan and often exchanged the poems he'd written with the Moody Bible Institute musician. In 1923, he was inspired by Lamentations 3:22-23 to write the text for the hymn, "Great is thy Faithfulness". Those verses declare, "The steadfast love of the Lord never ceases, his mercies never come to an end; they are new every morning; great is your faithfulness." (RSV) Runyan was so moved by this poem that Chisholm sent to him that he decided to compose a melody to go with the lyrics. Chisholm explained the poem in this way: "My income has not been large at any time due to impaired health which has followed me until now. Although I must not fail to record the unfailing faithfulness of a covenant-keeping God and that He has given me many wonderful displays of His providing care, for which I am filled with astonishing gratefulness." Runyan wrote of the hymn: "This particular poem held such an appeal that I prayed most earnestly that my tune might carry over its message in a worthy way, and the subsequent history of its use indicates that God answered prayer." Runyan had it sung so often at chapel services that the song became the unofficial theme song of the college. Runyan was a friend of Dr. Will Houghton, the president of Moody Bible Institute, and "Great is thy Faithfulness" soon became Houghton's favorite. He invited George Beverly Shea, an unknown singer at the time, to sing hymns on the Institute's radio station. Shea, of course, included Houghton's favorite hymn in his repertoire. Through those radio broadcasts Billy Graham, then a student at Wheaton College, became familiar with George Beverly Shea and the song, "Great is thy Faithfulness". Graham asked Shea to become part of his ministry of evangelism, and in 1945, George Beverly Shea began to sing the song at the Billy Graham Crusades, gaining it further exposure and popularity. Shea introduced Chisholm's hymn during the evangelistic meetings in Great Britain in 1954, and it immediately became a favorite and defining memory of the crusade that year. It was through these crusades that this hymn became internationally popular. In retirement, Chisholm continued to write poems and hymns, as he had throughout his life. Altogether he wrote over 1,200 poems and hymns. His writings often appeared in religious periodicals. Thomas Chisholm died in 1960 at the age of 93.

112 - TRUST AND OBEY

The hymn was inspired in 1886 during one of Dwight L. Moody's famous revivals. His music partner, Ira D. Sankey, shared: "Mr. Moody was conducting meetings in Brockton, Massachusetts, and I had the pleasure of singing for him. One night a young man rose in a testimony meeting and said, 'I am not quite sure - but I am going to trust, and I am going to obey.' I just jotted that sentence down and sent it with a little story to a Presbyterian pastor friend, John Sammis. He wrote the hymn, and the tune was born."The hymn first appeared in a collection of hymns in 1887 and has been included in many hymnals since then. Sammis was born in Brooklyn, N.Y., and was a businessman in Indiana. Working with the YMCA, he was later called to the ministry, attended McCormick and Lane Seminaries, and was ordained as a Presbyterian minister in 1880. After serving several congregations, he joined the faculty of the Los Angeles Bible Institute, where he taught until his death. John wrote a handful of hymns, the most popular of which is "Trust and Obey". It shares the rewards that come from trusting God's Word and obeying God's will. Our eternal reward will be when "in fellowship sweet we will sit at his feet".

113 - SAVIOR, LIKE A SHEPHERD LEAD US

"Savior, Like a Shepherd Lead Us" is attributed to Dorothy Thrupp and appears in most Christian hymnals. Dorothy was born in London, England in 1799 and died there in 1847. She spent her entire life in London, where she wrote stories for children's magazines. Avoiding publicity and using pen names, Dorothy was not well known for her works, and we know little about how this hymn was written. Since the focus of the original song was young children, Thrupp wanted to include the message of a caring Christ who loves all his children. Christ is pictured as a shepherd offering care and guidance to his flock as well as preparing for service and Christian life. This is followed by an acknowledgement that we belong to Christ. Thrupp includes hints of Psalm 23 as well as the picture of Christ as the Good Shepherd from John 10. There is one remarkable story in connection with this hymn that adds preciousness to the song. Ira Sankey was the famous song leader for D. L. Moody, and in his autobiography, Sankey shared this story: "The year was 1876, and Sankey was traveling on a steamboat up the Delaware River on Christmas Eve. Travelers on such a holiday, seemingly cut adrift in a world where everyone else is celebrating with loved ones, often seem to cling together making a circle of warmth in a waiting room, in a plane, or in an almost deserted restaurant. It was such a journey. On the deck were gathered a number of passengers, looking out at the calm, starlit night. Someone said, 'Mr. Sankey is aboard!', and immediately there were cries of 'Let him sing for us! Let's ask Mr. Sankey to sing!' He stood leaning against one of the great funnels of the boat. Before he began, he stood for a moment as if in prayer, deciding what to sing. He wanted to sing a Christmas song, but somehow the words of the Shepherd Song were what came to his heart.

'Savior, like a shepherd lead us,Much we need thy tender care.In thy pleasant pastures feed us,For our use thy folds prepare.'

Among the listeners, there was a deep stillness. The words telling the sweet story of God's love for wandering men, and the beautiful melody floated out across the deck, across the water, into the night. Every heart was stirred. At the end of the song, there was an almost audible response. One man stepped forth - a rough-looking man. To Sankey, he said, 'Did you ever serve in the Union Army?'

'Yes', answered Sankey, 'in the spring of 1860'.

'Can you remember if you were doing picket duty on a bright moonlight night in 1862?'

'Yes, I do', answered Sankey, with surprise. 'Were you...?'

'I did, too, but I was serving in the Confederate Army. When I saw you standing at your post, I said to myself, 'That fellow will never get away from here alive.' I raised my musket and took aim. I was in the shadow, completely hidden, while you walked in full moonlight.

'At that instant, you began to sing - just as a moment ago. The song was 'Savior, like a shepherd lead us...'

'The music reached my heart. I took my finger off the trigger. 'I'll wait until the end of the song,' I said to myself. 'I can't miss him, and I can shoot him afterwards.'

'As you sang, you reached the place where it says,'We are Thine, do Thou befriend us,"Be the guardian of our way..."

'I could hear every word perfectly, and how the memories came to my heart! I began to think of my childhood and my mother. She loved God. She had sung that song to me many times. But she died all too soon, otherwise I think my life might have been different. At the end of the song, I could not raise my musket again. It was impossible for me to take aim, though you still stood in the bright moonlight, a perfect target. Then I thought of the Lord. I looked at you and thought, 'The Lord who was able to save that man from certain death must surely be great and mighty.' My arm dropped to my side and I cannot tell you all the things I thought at that time. My heart was smitten, but I didn't know what to do. Just now, when you were about to sing and stood quietly as if praying, I recognized you. I've wandered far and wide, since that other occasion. I have never found that Shepherd. Please help me now find a cure for my sick soul.'

Deeply moved, Mr. Sankey threw his arms about the man who had been his enemy, who, indeed, could have ended his life. That Christmas Eve night, a former soldier found the great and tender Shepherd as his Savior. On a riverboat going up the Delaware River on Christmas Eve 1876, Ira Sankey suddenly realized how blessed a man he was to have sung these words back in 1862 on that moonlit evening."

114 - DAY BY DAY

As a child, Carolina Sandell spent her hours playing quietly in her Lutheran father's study as he worked on sermons in Froderyd, Sweden. Born on October 3, 1832, Lina grew up to become Sweden's best known author of Gospel hymns. She wrote over 650 hymns during her lifetime. Like many Christians, Lina learned that when pain or tragedy strike, God may use that experience to deepen our faith. When she was 26, Lina experienced a tragedy which greatly affected the rest of her life. She was with her father on a ferry crossing Lake Vattern in Sweden. As the boat sailed across the large lake on its way to Gothenburg, Pastor Sandell and his daughter stood on the deck and were enjoying the view. They had always shared a close, loving relationship. As a child, Lina had been sickly and often stayed close to her father while the other children played outside. Not only did those hours together build a special bond between them, but through her father's tender, loving example, she learned to know the sweet compassion and care of her Heavenly Father. As she grew older, she became her father's secretary, and that was why she was accompanying him on this boat trip. They were on the deck leaning against the rail enjoying the beauty of the day. Suddenly the ship lurched, and in front of her eyes, her father was thrown overboard and drowned before anyone was able to rescue him. She wrote this hymn sometime after that tragic event. Its words express how dependent she was on the Lord to carry her through this tragedy. Lina had written hymns before, but now she poured out her heart with a succession of beautiful songs. Her hymns greatly influenced the revival that swept across Scandinavia in the late 1800s. Of all her hymns, this is the one for which she is best known. Her words reflect the meditations of her own heart. "Day by Day" was brought to America by Swedish immigrants, some of who planted First Swedish Baptist Church in Minneapolis. It was eventually renamed Bethlehem Baptist Church, which later was John Piper's church.

115 - LIKE A RIVER GLORIOUS

Francis Ridley Havergal was born in Astley, England on December 14, 1836. As a teenager, she said, "I committed my soul to the Savior, and earth and heaven seemed brighter from that moment." In 1860, she left Worcester and lived in several places after that. As a single woman, Frances Havergal was also often sick, and her body was weak. But her faith and trust in God were strong, so that she was able to live in thankfulness to God. In 1876, while on vacation in Wales, she caught a cold that developed into a severe inflammation. As she became weaker, she was told that she might die. But her reaction surprised her friends. She stated, "If I am really going, it is too good to be true." However, she soon recovered and began to write a hymn describing the peace God had given her called, "Like a River Glorious". She knew he promised to provide "peace like a river," a "perfect peace" to those who focused on him and trusted in him (Isaiah 26:3). As she herself had experienced, God's perfect peace flows "like a river". It flows "fuller every day" and grows "deeper all the way". No matter what life may bring our way, we can trust God. As Havergal wrote, when we focus on him, our hearts can find "perfect peace and rest". Frances was often called "England's Consecration Poet" because of her daily walk with God. Not only was her life dedicated to him, but before she wrote any poetry she would seek God's face; then she would remember to give him glory for her new poem. She died at Caswell Bay, Swansea, on June 3, 1879. Reverend James Davidson said this about her life and her writings: "Miss Havergal's scholastic requirements were extensive, embracing several modern languages, together with Greek and Hebrew. She does not occupy, and did not claim for herself, a prominent place as a poet, but by her distinct individuality she carved out a niche which she alone could fulfill. Simply and sweetly she sang the love of God, and his way of salvation. To this end, and for this object, her whole life and all her powers were consecrated. She lives and speaks in every line of her poetry. Her poems are permeated with the fragrance of her passionate love of Jesus. The burden of her writings is a free and full salvation through the Redeemer's merits, for every sinner who will receive it, and her life was devoted to the proclamation of this truth by personal labors, literary efforts, and earnest interest in foreign missions."

116 - THOU WHO WAST RICH BEYOND ALL SPLENDOR

This hymn was written during a period of turmoil, unrest, and persecution in the history of missions in China. Following the anti-foreigner uprising known as the Boxer Rebellion, further upheaval and change was occurring across the land. Many missionaries were pursued or captured by the Communist army. My grandfather was also nearly executed when he was stood up against a wall to be shot but managed to escape when the soldiers' attention was diverted elsewhere. Some missionaries were released after a while, others were never heard from again. In 1934 missionaries John and Betty Stam were captured in Anhwei province and beheaded. Frank Houghton, who worked with the China Inland Mission at the time, wrote the hymn following the martyrdom of these two missionaries. Eventually, all of the foreign missionaries were forced to leave China, including my grandparents, Lewis and Eliza Lancaster. What Hudson Taylor and others had begun almost 100 years before would be left to the Chinese Christians to continue. John and Betty Stams' great-nephew, Chip Stam, shared this story of that time: "The news of these sorrows had reached the mission's headquarters in Shanghai. Though this was a very dangerous time for both the Chinese Christians and the foreign missionaries, Frank Houghton decided he needed to begin a tour through the country to visit various missionary outposts. While traveling over the mountains of Szechwan, the powerful and comforting words of 2 Corinthians 8:9 (though he was rich, yet for your sake he became poor), were transformed into this beautiful Christmas hymn."

117 - MORE LOVE TO THEE, O CHRIST

This text was written by Elizabeth Prentiss, who was born in Portland, Maine, on October 26, 1818. At age 16, she began writing, and some of her works were published in a Boston magazine. During her life, she produced over 100 poems, along with some novels and devotional works. Her most famous book was "Stepping Heavenward", which is still in print. After receiving her education, she taught school in Portland, as well as in Massachusetts and Virginia. In 1845, at age 27, she married George Prentiss, a minister. They had two children and relocated to New York City, where Mr. Prentiss served as the pastor of the Mercer St. Presbyterian Church and taught homiletics at Union Theological Seminary. The Prentisses were enjoying their life in New York, and by 1851 had two children, Annie and Eddy, with a third child on the way. But Eddy became ill in November of that year, and passed away in January. Bessie was born three months later, but the following month she also died suddenly during an epidemic. One evening when they returned from putting flowers on their children's graves, Elizabeth talked about her "unutterable longings to flee from a world that has had for me so many sharp experiences". When she questioned the reality of the love of God, George replied softly, "But it is in times like these that God loves us all the more, just as we loved our own children more when they were sick or troubled or in distress." He encouraged his wife to return God's love. Elizabeth later went to her room to read and meditate on her Bible and hymnbook. She thought about the story of Jacob and noticed the hymn based on it by Sarah Adams, "Nearer My God, to Thee". Thinking along the same line, the words, "More love, to Thee, O Christ", came to her mind, and Mrs. Prentiss began writing. She quickly penned the beginning words to the hymn; however, she thought so little of the poem that she did not show it to anyone for over ten years. The last line was added before it was printed, and it was finally published in 1869. The song quickly became very popular. Elizabeth's life was full of difficulties, including a body wracked with pain, and for much of her life she lived almost as an invalid. During these trying times she had to refocus her life from doing to being: "I see now that to live for God, whether one is allowed to be actively useful or not, is a great thing, and that it is a wonderful mercy to be allowed even to suffer, if thereby one can glorify Him." Though she was nearly incapacitated, Mrs. Prentiss continued to publish from time to time, producing several books before her death in 1878. Loss and sorrow often are the circumstances that lead to hymns being written. That was the case with "More Love to Thee". When Elizabeth died at the age of 59, it was sung at her funeral. George Prentiss later wrote a memoir of her life and commented on her reaction to the tragedies of 1852: "Although the death of these two children tore with anguish the mother's heart, she made no show of grief, and to the eye of the world her life soon appeared to move on as before. Never again, however, was it exactly the same life. She had entered into the fellowship of Christ's sufferings, and the new experience wrought a great change in her whole being." Elizabeth had asked her husband, "Why should this happen to us, of all people?" He had replied, "Maybe we should ask ourselves why a thing like this should not happen to us. Are we better than any of the other families who have lost loved ones in this epidemic?"

118 - O JESUS, I HAVE PROMISED

John Ernest Bode was an Anglican pastor who studied at Oxford and then ministered near Cambridge, England during the 1800s. When his three children were ready for confirmation in the church, Bode wrote this hymn especially for the occasion - telling his children that the hymn included "all the important truths I want you to remember". The hymn is an appropriate statement of commitment for any believer. It reminds us of the promises we are making to Jesus and asks him to protect us from the dangers and temptations we encounter in the world - and reminds us that Jesus has promised that we will live with him in glory. It caught on and became so popular that the Church of England told ministers to stop using it so excessively for confirmation services. Bode wrote poetry and hymns throughout his life, but this is his best known song.

119 - I LOVE THY KINGDOM, LORD

This is the only hymn from America's earliest days until the beginning of the nineteenth century that is still sung today. The writer of it, Timothy Dwight, is well known from early American history. Dwight was born in Northampton, Massachusetts in 1752. Like his grandfather, Jonathan Edwards, Timothy Dwight was a brilliant scholar. He could read Latin when he was 6 years old, graduated from Yale at 17, began teaching there at 19, and wrote his first book at 20. He wrote 33 hymns, with this being his best known one. It was published in 1800 at the beginning of the Second Great Awakening as part of an edition of Isaac Watts' Psalms. Dwight's hymn was used for evangelism as well as to comfort believers. He enlisted in the Continental Army in 1777 as a chaplain, where he became known for writing songs to encourage the troops, and for a while he served as a chaplain for George Washington. After the war, Dwight settled in Northampton, where he was a farmer, preacher, student, and representative in the state legislature. After later becoming a Congregational minister in Fairfield, Connecticut, Dwight also opened a private academy, whose success led to his election in 1795 as President of Yale College. Dwight left a legacy of improved academics at Yale, serving not only as the school's President, but also as professor of literature, oratory and theology, and college chaplain. While he was there, he also brought a spiritual emphasis to the campus. Before that, the students at Yale had been influenced by modernist ideas, and there were only a handful of Christians on campus. His leadership brought a spiritual revival which spread to other college campuses as well. Dwight's prolific writings included five volumes of sermons titled "Theology Explained and Defended". In the last 40 years of his life, Dwight contracted smallpox, affecting his eyesight. The pain in his eyes was severe and constant. Though being able to read for only a few minutes at a time, he persisted in writing books and hymns.

Made in the USA
Columbia, SC
29 July 2024

39154704R10145